Essentials of
NEW TESTAMENT GREEK

Essentials of

NEW TESTAMENT GREEK

Ray Summers

Chairman, Department of Religion
Baylor University
Waco, Texas

BROADMAN PRESS
Nashville, Tennessee

Copyright, 1950
BROADMAN PRESS
Nashville, Tennessee

17th Printing

ISBN: 0-8054-1309-x
4213-09

Printed in the United States of America

To

My Greek Teachers
J. W. Crowder
L. R. Elliott
H. E. Dana

CONTENTS

INTRODUCTION

Multiplied volumes have been written on the history of the Greek language and its place in the cultural life of the world. For the purpose at hand it is sufficient to indicate that the Greek of the New Testament is the language which was commonly used in the Greek-speaking world from the time of Alexander the Great to about A.D. 500. For this reason it is called *Koine* or common Greek in distinction from the classical Greek of the world of letters. God's written revelation of his Son was given in the language of the people. It was the logical medium for this revelation because it is the most expressive language known to man.

The course of study often employed is the presentation of the forms of Greek in a beginner's course followed by an advanced study of the function of Greek forms. It is the belief of this writer that it is possible to teach Greek forms (inflection) and at the same time teach the basic function of the forms, i.e., the significance of cases, tenses, voices, moods, etc., of the language. Such a course should be followed in the second year of study by extensive reading in the Greek New Testament with appeals to more mature work on the matter of grammatical and syntactical significance; such work as is represented by Dana and Mantey, *A Manual Grammar of the Greek New Testament,* and the all-time classic in the field: Robertson, *A Grammar of the Greek New Testament in the Light of Historical Research.* This procedure will eliminate the non-credit year of Greek study many times used in lieu of a year of college Greek and at the same time give the student wide reading in the Greek text, which is absolutely essential if the student is to learn to use his Greek New Testament. This book is the outgrowth of the application of the method in the classroom. The result has been most gratifying.

LESSON 1

SOME GENERAL MATTERS OF IMPORTANCE

1. The Greek Alphabet

Capital Letters	Small Letters	Name	Pronunciation
A	α	Alpha	a as in father (long) / a as in bat (short)
B	β	Beta	b as in ball
Γ	γ[1]	Gamma	g as in gift
Δ	δ	Delta	d as in debt
E	ε	Epsilon	e as in met
Z	ζ	Zeta	dz as in adz
H	η	Eta	e as in obey
Θ	θ	Theta	th as in theme
I	ι	Iota	i as in magazine (long) / i as in pit (short)
K	κ	Kappa	k as in kin
Λ	λ	Lambda	l as in long
M	μ	Mu	m as in man
N	ν	Nu	n as in no
Ξ	ξ	Xi	x as in relax
O	ο	Omicron	o as in omelet
Π	π	Pi	p as in pay
P	ρ	Rho	r as in ring
Σ	σ, ς[2]	Sigma	s as in sing
T	τ	Tau	t as in tale

[1]Before another γ, or before κ or χ, γ is pronounced ng, i.e., ἄγγελος (angel).
[2]ς is used when Sigma is at the end of the word, elsewhere σ is used.

1

Υ	υ	Upsilon	u as in unity
Φ	φ	Phi	ph as in phonetics
Χ	χ	Chi	ch as in chemical
Ψ	ψ	Psi	ps as in taps
Ω	ω	Omega	o as in tone

2. Writing the Greek Letters

Help from an instructor is indispensable in learning to write the Greek letters. The following suggestions may be helpful.

These letters are written on the line α ε ι κ ν ο π σ τ υ ω.

These letters are written partly on and partly below the line: γ η μ ρ ς χ.

These letters are written partly on and partly above the line: δ θ λ.

These letters are written on, above, and below the line: β ζ ξ φ ψ.

Capitals are used only to begin proper nouns; sentences begin with small letters.

3. The Vowels

These are the Greek vowels with their English equivalents: α (*a*), ε (short *e*), η (long *e* but pronounced more like *a* as in late), ο (short *o*), ι (*i*), υ (*u*), and ω (long *o*).

Of these vowels, ε and ο are always short; η and ω are always long; α, ι, and υ may be either long or short; only by observation will the student be able to determine the tone quality of α, ι, and υ.

α, ε, ο, η, and ω are pronounced with the mouth well open and are called *open* vowels. ι and υ are pronounced with the mouth nearly closed and are called *close* vowels.

4. The Diphthongs

As in English two vowels often unite in a syllable to form a single sound. Such a construction is called a *diphthong*. They are formed by the combination of an *open* and a *close* vowel (in that order) except in the case of υι which is formed by the two *close* vowels. The common or proper diphthongs are as follows:

2

αι, pronounced like ai in *aisle*

ει, pronounced like ei in *height* (some grammars indicate "a" as
    in late)

οι, pronounced like oi in *oil*

αυ, pronounced like au in *kraut*

ευ, pronounced like eu in *feud*

ου, pronounced like ou in *group*

υι, pronounced like *wee*

In addition to these there are some rare or "improper" diphthongs, ηυ and ωυ, which are pronounced by sounding the two
letters very close together rather than giving each one a distinct
sound; for example āū and ōū.

The *iota*-subscript diphthongs have no parallel in English.
There were times when ι followed long α, η, or ω but in the
development of the Greek language had become mute. It is so
persistent a letter that it refused to be lost even though it was
not sounded. In such cases it dropped back under long α, η, or ω
and became ι-subscript (ᾳ, ῃ, ῳ). These diphthongs are always
long in tone and are pronounced just like long α, η, and ω; the
sound of the vowel is not altered by the presence of the ι
subscript.

All diphthongs are long in tone except αι and οι when they
are final in the word.[1] When they are final — having no other
letter following them — they are considered short for purposes
of accenting. The sound is unchanged; final αι (or οι) is pronounced just like non-final αι (or οι). Hence, οι in ἄνθρωποι
is short because it is final; οι in ἀνθρώποις is long because it is
followed by another letter. By the same token in οἶκοι the first
οι is long and the second is short, while in οἴκοις both syllables
are long.

5. The Consonants

The consonants of the Greek alphabet are divided into three
general classes. The "liquid" consonants are pronounced by a
smooth, easy flow of breath. The "mute" consonants are pro-

---

[1] In the optative mood αι and οι are long even when final.

nounced by a momentary closing of the oral passage. The "sibilants" are those consonants having the "s" sound.

Liquid consonants: λ, μ, ν, ρ.

Mute Consonants:	Smooth	Middle	Rough
Palatal (guttural)	κ	γ	χ
Labial	π	β	φ
Dental	τ	δ	θ

Note: In pronouncing these letters the oral passage experiences a momentary closure at some part. With the *palatal* (or guttural) consonants the back part of the throat is closed, i.e., at the soft palate. Practice closing the throat at that point and then making the sound. The *labial* consonants are pronounced by the closing of the oral passage at the lips. Close the lips and then "explode" them open with the sound. The *dental* consonants are pronounced by a closing of the oral passage at the teeth. Press the tip of the tongue firmly against the back of the upper teeth. Now pronounce the letters by forcing the tongue to break away from the teeth. Some of the letters of the mute class are sounded by a more pronounced closure of the oral passage than others; hence the designations smooth, middle, and rough.

Sibilant consonants: ζ, ξ, σ, ψ. Three of these are called double consonants. ζ is a combination of δ + ς; ξ is a combination of κ, γ, or χ + ς; ψ is a combination of π, β, or φ + ς.

6. Breathing Marks

Every Greek word beginning with a vowel or a diphthong must have a *breathing* mark. Initial ρ always has the rough breathing mark, i.e., ῥῆμα. The breathing mark is placed over the single vowel which opens a word or over the second vowel of a diphthong which opens a word, i.e., ἄνθρωπος, αὐτός.

There are two breathing marks in Greek. The smooth breathing is indicated by this mark ᾿ ; the rough breathing is indicated by this mark ῾ and calls for an h-sound to begin the word. Thus we see that ἤδη is pronounced *ádā*, while ἡμέρα is pronounced *hāméra.* By the same token the preposition ἐν is pronounced *en,* while the numeral ἕν is pronounced *hen.* There are no rules to indicate which breathing mark is to be used. That is a matter of the spelling of the word and must be learned as a part of correct vocabulary study.

7. Accent Marks

There are three accent marks in Greek. Like the breathing marks these accent marks stand over vowels (never consonants) and over the second vowel in the case of a diphthong.

In their speech the Greeks used rising and falling voice inflection. This was indicated by the accent mark in the written language. An acute accent mark (') indicated pronunciation with a rising inflection of voice. A grave accent (`) indicated a falling inflection on final syllables in certain constructions. A circumflex accent (ˆ) was a combination of the rising and falling inflections. For practical purposes today we do not try to reproduce this inflection. We stress the syllable which is accented. All Greek words have an accent mark except proclitics and enclitics which will be learned at the proper time.

When a breathing mark and an accent stand on the same syllable, the breathing mark stands in front of the accent if it is acute, and under the accent if it is circumflex, i.e., οἴκου, οἶκος.

8. Punctuation Marks

In Greek there are four punctuation marks. The comma (,) and period (.) correspond to the English comma and period and are written on the line. The colon (·) corresponds to the English colon or semi-colon and is written above the line. The question mark (;) is made like the English semi-colon.

5

LESSON 2

ACCENT

9. Lexical Study

ἄγω,	I lead	ἄγγελος, ὁ,	messenger
ἀκούω,	I hear	ἀδελφός, ὁ	brother
βλέπω,	I see	δοῦλος, ὁ,	slave, servant
ἔχω,	I have	καρπός, ὁ,	fruit
λύω,	I loose,	λόγος, ὁ	word
	or I destroy		

Learn to pronounce these words stressing the syllable which carries the accent mark. The letter ὁ following the nouns indicates that the noun is masculine. This should be learned as a part of the vocabulary. Learn to spell the words by writing them out and accenting them correctly. Pronunciation will be aided by transliterating the words into English, i.e., λύω (*lúo*), ἄγγελος (*ángelos*), etc.

10. Grammatical Study

It is readily noticed that every word in the above section has an accent mark. The accent appears on different syllables as we move from one word to another. This introduces us to the Greek system of accent, which at first appearance seems quite complicated. There are some principles of accent, however, which when mastered make the system relatively simple. There are some preliminary observations which must be remembered.

First, *a Greek word has as many syllables as it has vowels or diphthongs.* The two vowels of a diphthong make *one* syllable not *two.* Thus we see that λόγος has two syllables, ἀδελφός has three syllables, δοῦλος has two syllables, etc. There is no rule for dividing a Greek word into syllables as far as the consonants are concerned. A convenient method is to begin with the beginning of the word and let the vowel which constitutes the syllable carry as many consonants as can be easily pronounced. For example, the following are easily pronounced divisions: ἄ-γω, βλέ-πω, καρ-πός. It would make no essential difference to divide as follows: ἄγ-ω, βλέπ-ω, καρπ-ός, etc. The essential thing is the vowel which constitutes the syllable, not the consonants pronounced with it.

Second, *a syllable is long if it has a long vowel or a diphthong.* For instance in βλέπω, βλε- is a short syllable while -πω is a long syllable; and in δοῦλος, δου- is a long syllable while -λος is a short syllable. The exception to this has been noted in the αι and οι diphthongs when they are final. Review this in the discussion on diphthongs (paragraph 4).

Third, *the names of the three important syllables are antepenult, penult, and ultima.* The ultima is the last syllable in the word, the penult is the next to the last, and the antepenult is the third from the last, i.e., the one before the penult. Thus in the word ἀδελφός, the ultima is -φος, the penult is -δελ-, and the antepenult is ἀ-. For purposes of accenting, syllables other than the last three are of no importance. Thus in ἀπολαμβάνομεν we have a word of six syllables, but for accent purposes we are concerned only with the last three since the Greek accent never went back beyond the third syllable from the end.

(1) General Rules of Accent

Accent in Greek was determined by the principle of sustained tone. The acute accent could sustain the tone three syllables, the circumflex two syllables, and the grave one syllable only. The result of this will be observed in the following rules.

1. The *acute* accent

   a. The acute accent can stand on either *short* or *long* syllables. λόγος, οἴκοις.
   b. The acute accent can stand on either of the last three syllables. ἄγγελος, λόγος, καρπός.
   c. The acute accent cannot stand on the antepenult when the

7

ultima is long. ἄγγελος is correct, but with a long ultima ἀγγέλου is correct.

d. The acute accent cannot stand on a long penult before a short ultima. δούλου is correct, but δούλος would be incorrect; it must be δοῦλος.

2. The *circumflex* accent

a. The circumflex accent can stand on *long* syllables only: δοῦλος, but not λόγος.

b. The circumflex accent can stand on either of the last two syllables, penult or ultima: δοῦλος or καρποῦ.

c. The circumflex accent cannot stand on the penult if the ultima is long. δοῦλος is correct, but δοῦλου is incorrect; it must be δούλου.

d. The circumflex accent must stand on an accented long penult before a short ultima. Thus δούλος would be incorrect; δοῦλος is correct.

3. The *grave* accent

The acute accent on the ultima changes to the grave accent when followed by other words without intervening marks of punctuation. ἀδελφός· is correct, but ἀδελφός δούλου is incorrect. In this construction the acute changes to the grave accent — ἀδελφὸς δούλου· This is the only use of the grave accent. The circumflex *never* changes to grave.

It is readily seen that these rules do not tell what accent a word will have. They tell the conditions under which the different accents may or may not be used. There are some special rules of accent which tell how any given word is to be accented.

(2) Noun Accent

Throughout a declension the accent in nouns remains on the same syllable as in the nominative singular as nearly as the general rules of accent permit. The position of the accent in the nominative singular (vocabulary form) must be learned as a part of the spelling of the word. When that is learned, the above rule takes care of the accent of the word. The following are the inflected forms of representative nouns. They are not to be learned now.

They are given to illustrate the above rule.

A	B	C	D
ἄγγελος	λόγος	δοῦλος	καρπός
ἀγγέλου	λόγου	δούλου	καρποῦ
ἀγγέλῳ	λόγῳ	δούλῳ	καρπῷ
ἄγγελον	λόγον	δοῦλον	καρπόν
ἄγγελοι	λόγοι	δοῦλοι	καρποί
ἀγγέλων	λόγων	δούλων	καρπῶν
ἀγγέλοις	λόγοις	δούλοις	καρποῖς
ἀγγέλους	λόγους	δούλους	καρπούς

A. The noun ἄγγελος begins in the nominative singular with the acute on the antepenult. The noun rule tells us that the accent remains on that syllable if the general rules do not forbid. But the general rules tell us that the acute cannot stand on the antepenult when the ultima is long. Therefore, in this word the acute will move over to the penult when the ultima becomes long, elsewhere it will be on the antepenult.

B. The noun λόγος begins with the acute accent on the penult. The noun rule tells us that the accent will remain on that syllable if the general rules do not forbid. There is nothing in the general rules to cause it to move from that syllable. The penult is short and can take only the acute accent; hence, the accent mark will not change position or form in the inflection of the word.

C. The noun δοῦλος begins the nominative singular with a circumflex on the penult. There is nothing in the general rules to cause the accent to move from that syllable so there will be no position change. There will be a form change, however, when the ultima becomes long because the circumflex cannot stand on the penult when the ultima is long.

D. The noun καρπός begins in the nominative singular with an acute on the ultima. The noun rule tells us the accent will remain on this syllable unless the general rules forbid. There is nothing in the general rules to cause it to change from the ultima. Therefore, there will be no position change of the accent. There will be a form change to circumflex in certain constructions, the reason for which will be learned later.

9

Careful study of these illustrations will make the noun accent a simple matter.

(3) Verb Accent

The accent in verbs is recessive. This means that in all verb forms the accent stands as far from the ultima as the general rules permit. Determine the tone (long or short) of the ultima, place the accent as far away as possible, and the matter is solved. Observe the following illustrations. Do not try to learn the forms yet.

λύω	λύομαι	ἐλυόμην
λύεις	λύῃ	ἐλύου
λύει	λύεται	ἐλύετο
λύομεν	λυόμεθα	ἐλυόμεθα
λύετε	λύεσθε	ἐλύεσθε
λύουσι	λύονται	ἐλύοντο

11. Practical Application

(1) Accent the following *noun* forms. The nominative singular form is correctly accented.

A. ἄνθρωπος	B. πλοῦτος	C. νόμος	D. αἶνος
ἀνθρωπου	πλουτου	νομου	αινου
ἀνθρωπῳ	πλουτῳ	νομῳ	αινῳ
ἀνθρωπον	πλουτον	νομον	αινον
ἀνθρωποι	πλουτοι	νομοι	αινοι
ἀνθρωπων	πλουτων	νομων	αινων
ἀνθρωποις	πλουτοις	νομοις	αινοις
ἀνθρωπους	πλουτους	νομους	αινους

(2) Accent the following *verb* forms.

A. λυω	B. λυομαι	C. ἐλυομην
λυεις	λυῃ	ἐλυου
λυει	λυεται	ἐλυετο
λυομεν	λυομεθα (short a)	ἐλυομεθα (short a)
λυετε	λυεσθε	ἐλυεσθε
λυουσι (short ι)	λυονται	ἐλυοντο

10

LESSON 3

VERBS: PRESENT ACTIVE INDICATIVE

12. Lexical Study

γινώσκω,	I know	λαμβάνω,	I take
γράφω,	I write	λέγω,	I say, I speak
διδάσκω,	I teach	πέμπω,	I send
ἐγείρω,	I raise up	φέρω,	I bear, I bring

13. Grammatical Study

The highly inflected nature of the Greek verb made it a marvelous implement in the expression of ideas. This inflection is noted in indicating the different elements which enter into the verbal idea. Like the verb in other languages the Greek verb has tense, voice, mood, person, and number.

Tense is the quality of the verb which has to do with action. There are two outstanding things in the matter of action, i.e., *time* of action and *kind* of action. As to *time* of action there are three possibilities: past, present, or future. As to *kind* of action there are (for present consideration) two possibilities: linear or punctiliar. Linear action is action regarded as a line (_____). It is also called progressive, or continuous action. Punctiliar action is action regarded as a point (.), i.e., action contemplated as a single perspective. Examples: linear action, "he is loosing"; punctiliar action, "he loosed."

The present tense indicates *progressive* action at the *present* time — "he is loosing." Kind and time of action in other tenses will be learned in subsequent lessons.

Voice is the quality of verbs which indicates the relationship

11

of the subject to the action. The active voice means that the subject is acting — "he is loosing." The passive voice means that the subject is being acted upon — "he is being loosed." These are the same in English and Greek. There is in Greek another voice (middle), the significance of which can best be learned later.

Mood is the quality of verbs which indicates the relation of the action to reality. Is the action conceived of as not really taking place but potential? Mood indicates this. For example, "he is loosing the dog" indicates that the action is really taking place. "Loose the dog" indicates that the action is not really taking place but is potential — it is possible for it to take place. There are several moods to express the idea of potential action in its various shades; these are for subsequent lessons. For the present it is sufficient to learn that the *indicative mood is that mood which confirms the reality of the action from the viewpoint of the speaker.*

Person is the quality of verbs which indicates whether the subject is speaking (first person), is being spoken to (second person), or is being spoken of (third person). For example, I am loosing (first), you are loosing (second), he (she or it) is loosing (third).

Number is the quality of verbs which indicates whether the subject is singular or plural. "I am loosing" (first singular). "We are loosing" (first plural), etc.

To analyze (or parse) the verb form λύω, we say it is present tense, active voice, indicative mood, first person, singular number. For practical usage say, "Present, active, indicative, first, singular." Apply the above description of the different elements and you have the complete story told by the simple form λύω.

(1) The present active indicative of λύω is:

λύω,	I loose or I am loosing	λύομεν,	we loose or we are loosing
λύεις,	you loose or you are loosing	λύετε,	you loose or you are loosing
λύει,	he (she or it) looses or is loosing	λύουσι,	they loose or they are loosing

No subject pronoun is needed. This is cared for by the inflected

12

ending (personal ending) of the verb. The use of subject pronouns in Greek is a special study for later observation. ἄνθρωπος λύει means "a man is loosing." λύει means "he is loosing."

(2) The stem of the verb is that part which remains unchanged through the process of inflection. To obtain the *present* stem of the verb, remove the ω from the first person singular (the vocabulary form). Thus we note that the present stem of λύω is λυ-, the present stem of λέγω is λεγ-, the present stem of γινώσκω is γινωσκ-, etc. The conjugation of the present active indicative of any verb in Lesson 2 or Lesson 3 may be formed by finding the stem and then adding the personal endings -ω, εις, ει, -ομεν, -ετε, -ουσι.

Originally the endings were different from these. In the early development of the language the endings were -μι, -σι, -τι, -μεν, -τε, -ντι. These were connected to the stem with what is called a "variable vowel" (ο before an ending beginning with μ or ν, ε before other endings). Hence the early forms were λύομι, λύεσι, λύετι, etc. As the language developed, these forms were gradually altered to the above forms. For the beginning student it is best to ignore the original forms and learn the endings as indicated -ω, -εις, -ει, -ομεν, -ετε, -ουσι.

(3) It should be noted that both the second person singular (λύεις) and the second person plural (λύετε) are translated "you are loosing." This is due to the fact that present English usage makes no distinction between these forms. In older translations of the Bible and in many Greek grammars the archaic "thou" (singular) and "ye" (plural) are used. This policy is not followed in this grammar because the expressions are so out of date. Close observation on the part of the student should eliminate confusion at this point.

14. Practical Application

(1) Translate the following:

1. ἄγει, ἀκούει, βλέπει, ἔχει. 2. λύομεν, γινώσκομεν, γράφομεν, διδάσκομεν. 3. ἐγείρουσι, λαμβάνουσι, λέγουσι, πέμπουσι. 4. φέρεις, φέρετε, ἄγομεν, ἀκούουσι. 5. γράφετε, γινώσκει, διδάσκουσι, λέγεις.

13

(2) Translate the following:

1. They see, he is leading, we take, you (pl.) hear. 2. I destroy, we raise up, you (sing.) are writing, he knows. 3. They send, we bring, he teaches, you (pl.) bring. 4. You (pl.) are leading, he is hearing, they raise up, we are seeing.

(3) Parse the following and translate:

1. γινώσκετε 2. ἔχομεν 3. ἄγουσι 4. λέγεις 5. ἐγείρει 6. ἀκούομεν 7. ἔχετε 8. βλέπουσι.

The different phases of this drill should be augmented by the teacher until he is certain that the matters of tense, voice, mood, person, and number are understood by the pupils.

LESSON 4

NOUNS: SECOND DECLENSION

15. Lexical Study

ἄνθρωπος, ὁ,	man	λίθος, ὁ,	stone
ἀπόστολος, ὁ,	apostle	νόμος, ὁ,	law
ἄρτος, ὁ,	bread, loaf	οἶκος, ὁ,	house
γάμος, ὁ,	marriage	ὄχλος, ὁ,	crowd,
δῶρον, τό,	gift		multitude
θάνατος, ὁ,	death	υἱός, ὁ,	son
ἱερόν, τό,	temple	καί,	conj., and

16. Grammatical Study

There are three declensions in Greek, i.e., three systems of inflecting Greek nouns. The first declension has an inflected system in which the *a* sound predominates; the second declension has a system in which the *o* sound predominates; and the third declension has a system in which consonant stems predominate. The largest number of Greek nouns is to be found in the second declension. For this reason, and because it is easier, it is studied first. The predominance of the *o* sound is observed in the inflected forms.

(1) Declension of ἄνθρωπος with the definite article:

	Singular	Plural
Nom.	ὁ ἄνθρωπος, the man	οἱ ἄνθρωποι, the men
Gen.	τοῦ ἀνθρώπου, of the man	τῶν ἀνθρώπων, of the men
Abl.	τοῦ ἀνθρώπου, from the man	τῶν ἀνθρώπων, from the men
Dat.	τῷ ἀνθρώπῳ, to the man	τοῖς ἀνθρώποις, to the men

15

Loc.	τῷ ἀνθρώπῳ, in the man	τοῖς ἀνθρώποις, in the men
Ins.	τῷ ἀνθρώπῳ, by the man	τοῖς ἀνθρώποις, by the men
Acc.	τὸν ἄνθρωπον, the man	τοὺς ἀνθρώπους, the men
Voc.	ἄνθρωπε, man	ἄνθρωποι, men

The article forms ὁ and οἱ are called proclitics. They are not accented and are pronounced very closely with the word which follows.

(2) There is no indefinite article in Greek. Thus we see that ἄνθρωπος means "man" or "a man." It does not, however, mean "the man" because Greek does have a definite article. The definite article for the masculine singular is ὁ. ὁ ἄνθρωπος means "the man." For the purpose of the exercises the student should observe this carefully. Do not insert an English "the" in translation unless the Greek article appears; do not insert a Greek "ὁ" unless the English "the" appears. There are times when the English article is used in translating a New Testament passage which has no Greek article. Reasons for this are of no concern here.

The Greek article is used to point out particular *identity*. This is called the "articular" use of a noun or other substantive. When no definite article is used with the noun (or other substantive), it is called the "anarthrous" use. The anarthrous construction is used to indicate quality or characteristics. For the present observe closely the use of the article and leave the significance of the anarthrous construction for a subsequent lesson.

(3) To parse a noun one must indicate four things about it: declension, case, gender, and number. Declension is a matter of inflected form and has no particular functional significance. The other three have to do with the function of the word.

Case has to do with the function of the noun as it relates to the verb or to other parts of the sentence. In Greek nouns there are four (five in some instances, i.e., where the vocative has a form separate from the nominative) inflected forms. There are, however, eight distinctive case functional ideas covered by these forms. The following chart indicates the forms, the case function, and the basic idea of each case.

16

Form	Case	Basic idea of the case
1. -ος (οι)	Nominative	Designation
2. -ου (ων)	Genitive	Description
	Ablative	Separation
3. -ῳ (οις)	Dative	Interest
	Locative	Location (or Position)
	Instrumental	Means
4. -ον (ους)	Accusative	Limitation
5. -ε (οι)	Vocative	Address

The forms given here are the forms of the second declension. The case and basic idea of the case are the same for all three declensions. The vocative, relatively rare in the new Testament, is often the same in form as the nominative. Further discussion of the separate cases is in order. This will indicate that *form* is a matter of *inflection* while *case* is a matter of *function*.

The *nominative* is the case of *designation*. It is the "naming" case. Its main use is that of subject of the sentence or clause. ὁ ἄνθρωπος γινώσκει is a Greek sentence in which the nominative serves as subject of the sentence. There is a variety of usage of this case, which will be observed in a subsequent lesson.

The *genitive* is the case of *description*. It is used to attribute quality to the word it modifies. ὁ οἶκος τοῦ ἀνθρώπου is a phrase in which the genitive ἀνθρώπου describes οἶκος by telling to whom it belongs — "the man's house," or "the house of the man." There are many other shades of description in the case usage. These, too, will be observed later.

The *ablative* is the case of *separation*. It uses the same *form* as the genitive but its function is distinct. ὁ ἄνθρωπος πέμπει τοὺς δούλους τοῦ οἶκου. "The man sends the servants *from the* house." τοῦ οἶκου is ablative indicating separation. Later there will be presented prepositions which assist the nouns to express their case function, but the case function is there without the preposition.

The *dative* is the case of *interest*. Its most frequent usage, though by no means its only one, is to express the indirect object of a verb. ὁ ἀπόστολος λέγει λόγους τοῖς ἀνθρώποις. "The apostle is saying words *to the men."* τοῖς ἀνθρώποις is the indirect object of λέγει.

The *locative* case is the case of *location* or *position.* It uses the same form as the dative. ὁ ἄνθρωπος διδάσκει τῷ οἴκῳ. "The man teaches *in the house."*

The *instrumental* case, which also uses the third inflected form, is the case which expresses *means.* ὁ ἄνθρωπος διδάσκει λόγοις. "The man teaches *with words."* This expresses the means by which the teaching is imparted.

The *accusative* case is the case of *limitation.* It marks the limit or the end of an action. The main usage is that of direct object of a verb. ὁ ἄνθρωπος λέγει λόγους. "The man is saying *words."*

The *vocative* case is the case of *address.* ἀδελφέ, βλέπω οἶκον. *"Brother,* I see a house." This case always takes the same form as the nominative in the plural. In the singular it varies in inflection from the nominative to a separate form. Its function is distinct from the nominative.

Gender in nouns indicates whether or not the noun is masculine, feminine, or neuter. Many words will parallel English usage at this point; the gender of others must be learned by observation as a part of the lexical study.

Number indicates whether the noun is one or more than one. *Koine* Greek has the same usage here as the English: *singular* for one, *plural* for two or more.

(4) Declension of other second declension masculine nouns. Compare the accenting of the word with ἄνθρωπος.

	Singular			Singular	
Nom.	ὁ λόγος,	the word	ὁ δοῦλος,	the slave
Gen.	τοῦ λόγου,	of the word	τοῦ δούλου,	of the slave
Abl.	τοῦ λόγου,	from the word	τοῦ δούλου,	from the slave
Dat.	τῷ λόγῳ,	to the word	τῷ δούλῳ,	to the slave
Loc.	τῷ λόγῳ,	in the word	τῷ δούλῳ,	in the slave
Ins.	τῷ λόγῳ,	by the word	τῷ δούλῳ,	by the slave
Acc.	τὸν λόγον,	—the word	τὸν δοῦλον,	—the slave
Voc.	λόγε,	word	δοῦλε,	slave

	Plural			Plural	
Nom.	οἱ λόγοι,	the words	Nom.	οἱ δοῦλοι,	the slaves
Gen.	τῶν λόγων,	of the words	Gen.	τῶν δούλων,	of the slaves
Abl.	τῶν λόγων,	from the words	Abl.	τῶν δούλων,	from the slaves
Dat.	τοῖς λόγοις,	to the words	Dat.	τοῖς δούλοις,	to the slaves
Loc.	τοῖς λόγοις,	in the words	Loc.	τοῖς δούλοις,	in the slaves
Ins.	τοῖς λόγοις,	by the words	Ins.	τοῖς δούλοις,	by the slaves
Acc.	τοὺς λόγους,	—the words	Acc.	τοὺς δούλους,	—the slaves
Voc.	λόγοι,	words	Voc.	δοῦλοι,	slaves

Any second declension noun with an acute accent on the antepenult will be accented like ἄνθρωπος; any with the acute on the penult will be accented like λόγος; any with the circumflex on the penult will be accented like δοῦλος; any with the acute on the ultima will be accented like υἱός which follows. This last is due to a special declension rule of accent: *An acute accent on the ultima in the nominative singular of second declension nouns changes to circumflex when the ultima becomes long except in the accusative* plural. Note how this accent rule is applied in υἱός (son) and καρπός (fruit).

	Singular		Singular
Nom.	ὁ υἱός		ὁ καρπός
Gen.	τοῦ υἱοῦ		τοῦ καρποῦ
Abl.	τοῦ υἱοῦ		τοῦ καρποῦ
Dat.	τῷ υἱῷ		τῷ καρπῷ
Loc.	τῷ υἱῷ		τῷ καρπῷ
Ins.	τῷ υἱῷ		τῷ καρπῷ
Acc.	τὸν υἱόν		τὸν καρπόν
Voc.	υἱέ		καρπέ

	Plural		Plural
Nom.	οἱ υἱοί		οἱ καρποί
Gen.	τῶν υἱῶν		τῶν καρπῶν
Abl.	τῶν υἱῶν		τῶν καρπῶν
Dat.	τοῖς υἱοῖς		τοῖς καρποῖς
Loc.	τοῖς υἱοῖς		τοῖς καρποῖς

Ins.	τοῖς υἱοῖς	τοῖς καρποῖς
Acc.	τοὺς υἱούς	τοὺς καρπούς

(5) Neuter nouns of the second declension differ from masculine nouns only in the nominative singular and the nominative and accusative plural. The accent principles are the same. The following are examples of neuter noun inflection. Note the difference in the inflection of the article.

	Singular		Singular
Nom. & Voc.[1]	τὸ δῶρον		τὸ ἱερόν
Gen.	τοῦ δώρου		τοῦ ἱεροῦ
Abl.	τοῦ δώρου		τοῦ ἱεροῦ
Dat.	τῷ δώρῳ		τῷ ἱερῷ
Loc.	τῷ δώρῳ		τῷ ἱερῷ
Ins.	τῷ δώρῳ		τῷ ἱερῷ
Acc.	τὸ δῶρον		τὸ ἱερόν

	Plural		Plural
Nom. & Voc.	τὰ δῶρα		τὰ ἱερά
Gen.	τῶν δώρων		τῶν ἱερῶν
Abl.	τῶν δώρων		τῶν ἱερῶν
Dat.	τοῖς δώροις		τοῖς ἱεροῖς
Loc.	τοῖς δώροις		τοῖς ἱεροῖς
Ins.	τοῖς δώροις		τοῖς ἱεροῖς
Acc.	τὰ δῶρα		τὰ ἱερά

Note: The plural ending "a" in second declension neuter nouns is *always* short.

(6) The normal word order in Greek is subject, verb, object, etc. This is not always followed. The order in the sentence is many times varied for purposes of emphasis or euphony. Word order is not a good guide in translation. Study the *endings* of the words closely for this purpose.

(7) For the purpose of euphony the Greek inserted the liquid consonant *ν* at the end of some words when they were followed

---

[1]Observe here and hereafter in these paradigms that the article is not to be used with the vocative case.

20

by a mark of punctuation or by a word beginning with a vowel. There are no *rules* for learning which words employed this device — the variety is too great. It can be learned only by observation. Outstanding in the usage is the third person plural of the present active indicative. Note: λέγουσιν ἀνθρώποις, but λέγουσι δούλοις. This construction is called "movable *ν*" and should be observed to avoid confusion in reading the Greek New Testament.

17. Practical Application

(1) Translate the following sentences:

1. ὁ ἄνθρωπος γινώσκει τὸν νόμον. 2. ὁ δοῦλος φέρει δῶρον. 3. ὁ ἄγγελος λέγει λόγον. 4. ἔχεις τὸν καρπόν. 5. οἱ ἀδελφοὶ ἀκούουσι τοὺς λόγους τοῦ ἀγγέλου. 6. πέμπετε δῶρα τῷ ἱερῷ. 7. βλέπομεν τοὺς οἴκους τῶν ὄχλων. 8. οἱ υἱοὶ τῶν ἀνθρώπων ἄγουσι τοὺς δούλους. 9. λαμβάνω δῶρα καρποῦ καὶ ἄρτου. 10. γράφομεν λόγους τοῖς ἀδελφοῖς. 11. βλέπω τὸν γάμον τῷ οἴκῳ. 12. οἱ ἄγγελοι γινώσκουσι θάνατον καὶ διδάσκουσιν ἀνθρώπους λόγοις. 13. οἱ ὄχλοι βλέπουσι τοὺς λίθους τῷ ἱερῷ καὶ τῷ οἴκῳ. 14. ὁ ἄγγελος λέγει λόγους θανάτου τοῖς ἀνθρώποις καὶ τοῖς υἱοῖς.

(2) Translate the following sentences:

1. The son has bread and fruit. 2. The brother speaks a word to the crowd. 3. You (singular) see stones in the houses and in the temples. 4. The servant is bearing a gift to the man. 5. We are hearing words of death from the messenger. 6. You (plural) are writing a word to the apostle. 7. Men, brothers, and sons are teaching the crowd. 8. He knows the word of the law. 9. You (singular) are seeing a crowd and a marriage in the house. 10. Servants speak words to the sons and bear gifts to the messengers.

21

LESSON 5

NOUNS: FIRST DECLENSION

18. Lexical Study

ἀγάπη, ἡ,	love	εἰρήνη, ἡ,	peace
ἀλήθεια, ἡ,	truth	ἐκκλησία, ἡ,	church
ἁμαρτία, ἡ,	sin	ἐντολή, ἡ,	commandment
βασιλεία, ἡ,	kingdom	ἡμέρα, ἡ,	day
γλῶσσα, ἡ,	tongue	μαθητής, ὁ,	disciple
γραφή, ἡ,	writing, Scripture	Μεσσίας, ὁ,	Messiah
διδαχή, ἡ,	teaching	παραβολή, ἡ,	parable
δόξα, ἡ,	glory	προφήτης, ὁ,	prophet

19. Grammatical Study

In the above vocabulary the article ἡ indicates that the nouns are feminine. It will be observed that all first declension nouns ending in α or η in the nominative singular are feminine. First declension nouns ending αs or ης in the nominative singular are masculine. The inflection of first declension nouns varies in the singular according to the ending in the nominative. The inflection in the plural of all first declension nouns is the same. This is called the α declension because of the predominance of the α sound.

Two special rules of declension accent must be observed here. The first is like the one learned in the second declension regarding the accent on the ultima. *The acute on the ultima in the nominative singular changes to circumflex when the ultima is long except in the accusative.* The second rule is new: *All first declen-*

sion nouns receive the circumflex on the ultima in the genitive and ablative plural no matter where the accent started in the nominative singular. Note the application of this rule in the paradigms to follow.

There are five systems of inflection in the singular of first declension nouns. The α in the accusative plural of all first declension nouns is *always* long.

(1) When the stem ends in ε, ι, or ρ, the nominative singular will end in long α, and this will be retained throughout the word. Note the feminine article. The ἡ and αἱ forms are proclitic.

	Singular		Singular
Nom. & Voc.	ἡ βασιλεία		ἡ ἡμέρα
Gen.	τῆς βασιλείας		τῆς ἡμέρας
Abl.	τῆς βασιλείας		τῆς ἡμέρας
Dat.	τῇ βασιλείᾳ		τῇ ἡμέρᾳ
Loc.	τῇ βασιλείᾳ		τῇ ἡμέρᾳ
Ins.	τῇ βασιλείᾳ		τῇ ἡμέρᾳ
Acc.	τὴν βασιλείαν		τὴν ἡμέραν

	Plural		Plural
Nom. & Voc.	αἱ βασιλεῖαι		αἱ ἡμέραι
Gen.	τῶν βασιλειῶν		τῶν ἡμερῶν
Abl.	τῶν βασιλειῶν		τῶν ἡμερῶν
Dat.	ταῖς βασιλείαις		ταῖς ἡμέραις
Loc.	ταῖς βασιλείαις		ταῖς ἡμέραις
Ins.	ταῖς βασιλείαις		ταῖς ἡμέραις
Acc.	τὰς βασιλείας		τὰς ἡμέρας

Note: The exception to this class is seen in a few words of which ἀλήθεια is an example. Here the α following ι is short in the nominative and accusative singular; elsewhere it is long.

(2) When the stem ends in σ, λλ, or one of the double consonants (paragraph 5), the nominative singular ends in short α, which changes to η in the second and third inflected forms singular, i.e., gen., abl., dat., loc., and ins.

23

	Singular	Singular
Nom. &		
Voc.	ἡ γλῶσσα	ἡ δόξα
Gen.	τῆς γλώσσης	τῆς δόξης
Abl.	τῆς γλώσσης	τῆς δόξης
Dat.	τῇ γλώσσῃ	τῇ δόξῃ
Loc.	τῇ γλώσσῃ	τῇ δόξῃ
Ins.	τῇ γλώσσῃ	τῇ δόξῃ
Acc.	τὴν γλῶσσαν	τὴν δόξαν

	Plural	Plural
Nom. &		
Voc.	αἱ γλῶσσαι	αἱ δόξαι
Gen.	τῶν γλωσσῶν	τῶν δοξῶν
Abl.	τῶν γλωσσῶν	τῶν δοξῶν
Dat.	ταῖς γλώσσαις	ταῖς δόξαις
Loc.	ταῖς γλώσσαις	ταῖς δόξαις
Ins.	ταῖς γλώσσαις	ταῖς δόξαις
Acc.	τὰς γλώσσας	τὰς δόξας

(3) When the stem ends in any other letter, the nominative singular will end in η, which is retained throughout the singular.

	Singular	Singular
Nom. &		
Voc.	ἡ γραφή	ἡ εἰρήνη
Gen.	τῆς γραφῆς	τῆς εἰρήνης
Abl.	τῆς γραφῆς	τῆς εἰρήνης
Dat.	τῇ γραφῇ	τῇ εἰρήνῃ
Loc.	τῇ γραφῇ	τῇ εἰρήνῃ
Ins.	τῇ γραφῇ	τῇ εἰρήνῃ
Acc.	τὴν γραφήν	τὴν εἰρήνην

	Plural	Plural
Nom. &		
Voc.	αἱ γραφαί	αἱ εἰρῆναι
Gen.	τῶν γραφῶν	τῶν εἰρηνῶν
Abl.	τῶν γραφῶν	τῶν εἰρηνῶν

Dat.	ταῖς γρυφαῖς	ταῖς εἰρήναις
Loc.	ταῖς γραφαῖς	ταῖς εἰρήναις
Ins.	ταῖς γραφαῖς	ταῖς εἰρήναις
Acc.	τὰς γραφάς	τὰς εἰρήνας

(4) When a masculine noun of the first declension has a stem ending in ε, ι, or ρ, the nominative singular will be ας (long α). All other stem endings are followed by ης in the nominative singular. Note the inflection of these masculine nouns.

	Singular	Singular
Nom. &		
Voc.	ὁ Μεσσίας	ὁ προφήτης (Voc. προφῆτα)
Gen.	τοῦ Μεσσίου	τοῦ προφήτου
Abl.	τοῦ Μεσσίου	τοῦ προφήτου
Dat.	τῷ Μεσσίᾳ	τῷ προφήτῃ
Loc.	τῷ Μεσσίᾳ	τῷ προφήτῃ
Ins.	τῷ Μεσσίᾳ	τῷ προφήτῃ
Acc.	τὸν Μεσσίαν	τὸν προφήτην

	Plural	Plural
Nom. &		
Voc.	οἱ Μεσσίαι	οἱ προφῆται
Gen.	τῶν Μεσσιῶν	τῶν προφητῶν
Abl.	τῶν Μεσσιῶν	τῶν προφητῶν
Dat.	τοῖς Μεσσίαις	τοῖς προφήταις
Loc.	τοῖς Μεσσίαις	τοῖς προφήταις
Ins.	τοῖς Μεσσίαις	τοῖς προφήταις
Acc.	τοὺς Μεσσίας	τοὺς προφήτας

(5) The Greek definite article has been given in full.

	Masculine	Feminine	Neuter
		Singular	
N.	ὁ	ἡ	τό
G. & A.	τοῦ	τῆς	τοῦ
D., L., & I.	τῷ	τῇ	τῷ
A.	τόν	τήν	τό

25

Plural

N.	οἱ	αἱ	τά
G. & A.	τῶν	τῶν	τῶν
D., L., & I.	τοῖς	ταῖς	τοῖς
A.	τούς	τάς	τά

20. Practical Application.

(1) Translate the following sentences:

1. ὁ ἀπόστολος διδάσκει παραβολὴν τοῖς ἀνθρώποις. 2. ὁ μαθητὴς βλέπει τὸν προφήτην τῇ ἐκκλησίᾳ. 3. ὁ ἄγγελος τοῦ Μεσσίου λέγει λόγους καὶ νόμους τοῖς ὄχλοις. 4. οἱ υἱοὶ τοῦ ἀνθρώπου γινώσκουσιν ἀγάπην καὶ ἀλήθειαν καὶ τὰς γραφάς. 5. ὁ προφήτης λέγει τοὺς λόγους παραβολῆς τῇ γλώσσῃ. 6. ὁ Μεσσίας ἔχει τὴν διδαχὴν δόξης καὶ εἰρήνης. 7. ὁ μαθητὴς γινώσκει ἁμαρτίαν καὶ λέγει λόγους ἀληθείας. 8. ὁ ἀπόστολος γράφει γραφὴν τῆς βασιλείας καὶ τῆς ἐκκλησίας. 9. οἱ υἱοὶ γινώσκουσι τὴν ἐντολὴν καὶ λέγουσι παραβολὴν τῷ οἴκῳ. 10. ὁ προφήτης λαμβάνει ἄρτον καὶ καρπὸν τοῦ υἱοῦ τοῦ μαθητοῦ. 11. ὁ ἄγγελος βλέπει τὸν Μεσσίαν καὶ γινώσκει τὴν ἡμέραν εἰρήνης. 12. ἀκούετε τὴν παραβολὴν τῆς βασιλείας καὶ γινώσκετε τὴν δόξαν ἀγάπης. 13. λέγομεν λόγους ἀληθείας ὄχλοις ἀνθρώπων καὶ μαθητῶν. 14. ἄγεις τοὺς ἀγγέλους καὶ λέγεις παραβολὴν τῆς ἐκκλησίας. 15. οἱ μαθηταὶ τῶν προφητῶν λύουσιν ἐκκλησίας καὶ ἱερὰ λίθοις.

(2) Translate the following sentences:

1. We know the parables of the kingdom and the teachings of the churches. 2. You (pl.) are hearing the words of the prophet and the commandments of the Messiah. 3. The disciples are writing Scriptures of love, peace, and truth to the crowds. 4. The man knows the sins of the sons. 5. The Messiah is teaching the teaching of glory and love. 6. We are hearing the parables of the church. 7. He is destroying churches with words and temples with stones. 8. The tongue of the prophet speaks the teaching of sin and the glory of truth. 9. The disciples are leading the men, and the men are hearing the Scriptures. 10. In the Messiah we have love and peace and truth. 11. They are taking bread and fruit from the houses and are bearing gifts to the crowds. 12. From commandments, laws, and words we know the teaching of the kingdom and of the churches of the Messiah.

LESSON 6

ADJECTIVES OF THE FIRST AND SECOND DECLENSIONS

21. Lexical Study

ἀγαθός, ή, όν, good
ἀγαπητός, ή, όν, beloved
ἄλλος, η, ο,[1] other, another
(usually "another of
the same kind")
βασιλικός, ή, όν, royal
δίκαιος, α, ον, righteous, just
ἔσχατος, η, ον, last
ἕτερος, α, ον, another (usually
"another of a differ-
ent kind")

καινός, ή, όν, new
κακός, ή, όν, bad
καλός, ή, όν, good,
beautiful
μικρός, ά, όν, small,
little
μόνος, η, ον, only, alone
νεκρός, ά, όν, dead
πιστός, ή, όν, faithful
πονηρός, ά, όν, evil
πρῶτος, η, ον, first

22. Grammatical Study

(1) Like nouns, adjectives have gender, number, and case. When they are used to modify nouns they must agree with their noun in gender, number, and case.

All the adjectives in the above vocabulary are adjectives which follow the analogy of the first and second declensions. The masculine and neuter follow the second declension; the feminine follows the first declension. All principles of accent are followed as in the respective declensions except the genitive and ablative plural feminine follow the regular noun rule rather than the special first declension rule. Note this in the paradigms below.

When the stem of the adjective ends in ε, ι, or ρ, the feminine

---
[1]This neuter form has no ν.

27

singular ending will be long α; otherwise it will be η. Learn the declension of the adjectives below; any adjectives of the first and second declensions will be declined after this pattern.

(2) Adjective Paradigms.

Singular

	M.	F.	N.	M.	F.	N.
N.	ἀγαθός	ἀγαθή	ἀγαθόν	μικρός	μικρά	μικρόν
G. & A.	ἀγαθοῦ	ἀγαθῆς	ἀγαθοῦ	μικροῦ	μικρᾶς	μικροῦ
D., L., & I.	ἀγαθῷ	ἀγαθῇ	ἀγαθῷ	μικρῷ	μικρᾷ	μικρῷ
A.	ἀγαθόν	ἀγαθήν	ἀγαθόν	μικρόν	μικράν	μικρόν
V.	ἀγαθέ	ἀγαθή	ἀγαθόν	μικρέ	μικρά	μικρόν

Plural

N. & V.	ἀγαθοί	ἀγαθαί	ἀγαθά	μικροί	μικραί	μικρά
G. & A.	ἀγαθῶν	ἀγαθῶν	ἀγαθῶν	μικρῶν	μικρῶν	μικρῶν
D., L., & I.	ἀγαθοῖς	ἀγαθαῖς	ἀγαθοῖς	μικροῖς	μικραῖς	μικροῖς
A.	ἀγαθούς	ἀγαθάς	ἀγαθά	μικρούς	μικράς	μικρά

Singular

N.	δίκαιος	δικαία	δίκαιον
G. & A.	δικαίου	δικαίας	δικαίου
D., L., & I.	δικαίῳ	δικαίᾳ	δικαίῳ
A.	δίκαιον	δικαίαν	δίκαιον
V.	δίκαιε	δικαία	δίκαιον

Plural

N. & V.	δίκαιοι	δίκαιαι	δίκαια
G. & A.	δικαίων	δικαίων	δικαίων
D., L., & I.	δικαίοις	δικαίαις	δικαίοις
A.	δικαίους	δικαίας	δίκαια

(3) The use of the adjectives.

Adjectives may be used in three distinct ways: attributively, predicatively, and substantivally.

The attributive use of the adjective is that in which the adjective *attributes a quality to the noun* modified. In this construction there are two possible positions of the adjective in relation to the noun: ὁ ἀγαθὸς λόγος, or ὁ λόγος ὁ ἀγαθός. Both constructions should be translated: "the *good* word." Note that the adjective is *immediately* preceded by the definite article in both constructions.[1] The predicate use of the adjective is that in which the adjective *makes an assertion* about the noun. Here, too, there are two possible positions of the adjective in relation to the noun: ὁ λόγος ἀγαθός, or ἀγαθὸς ὁ λόγος. Both constructions should be translated: "The word is good." Note that the adjective is *not immediately* preceded by the definite article.[1] This is a matter of tremendous importance in the interpretation of Greek. The following summary may help to keep the distinction in mind.

Attributive position $\left(\begin{array}{c} \text{ὁ ἀγαθὸς λόγος} \\ \text{or} \\ \text{ὁ λόγος ὁ ἀγαθός} \end{array} \right)$: "the good word"

Predicate position $\left(\begin{array}{c} \text{ὁ λόγος ἀγαθός} \\ \text{or} \\ \text{ἀγαθὸς ὁ λόγος} \end{array} \right)$: "The word is good."

The substantive use of the adjective is that in which the adjective is used as a noun. Thus ὁ ἀγαθός may mean "the good man," ἡ ἀγαθή may mean "the good woman," etc., without the use of a noun. Sometimes the masculine plural form is used in a more general way; hence, οἱ ἀγαθοί may mean "the good men" or "the good people" or simply "the good." In a similar way οἱ νεκροί may be "the dead men," "the dead people," or "the dead."

23. Practical Application

(1) Translate the following sentences:

1. ὁ ἀγαπητὸς μαθητὴς ἀκούει τοὺς ἀγαθοὺς λόγους. 2. ὁ βασιλικὸς νόμος διδάσκει τὴν δόξαν ἀγάπης. 3. ἀγαθὴ ἡ ἐκκλησία καὶ ἡ βασιλεία κακή. 4. ὁ Μεσσίας ἐγείρει τοὺς νεκρούς. 5. βλέπομεν τὸν κακὸν καρπὸν καὶ τὸν

---

[1] When no article is used, the context must determine whether the construction is attributive or predicate.

29

καλὸν ἄρτον. 6. οἱ προφῆται λέγουσι καινὰς παραβολὰς τοῖς πιστοῖς. 7. ὁ ἀπόστολος γινώσκει τοὺς δικαίους καὶ τὰς δικαίας. 8. οἱ πονηροὶ λέγουσι πονηροὺς λόγους ταῖς ἐσχάταις ἡμέραις. 9. ἀγαθὸς ὁ ἀδελφὸς καὶ διδάσκει τοὺς πιστοὺς τῇ ἐκκλησίᾳ. 10. οἱ δίκαιοι ἄνθρωποι γράφουσιν ἄλλην παραβολήν. 11. ὁ ἕτερος ἄνθρωπος ἔχει τὸν μόνον καλὸν οἶκον. 12. πιστὴ ἡ διδαχὴ καὶ ὁ νόμος δίκαιος.

(2) Translate the following sentences:

1. The brothers are first and the servants are last. 2. The son of the just man sees the beloved disciples. 3. The good women say good things. 4. The new fruit is good and the houses are bad. 5. The righteous are leading the evil men. 6. The Messiah knows the last days of the kingdom. 7. The evil men are destroying the other houses with small stones. 8. To the first church the apostle speaks the first parable. 9. The good things we say to the faithful men, and the bad things to the others. 10. Men are destroying the beautiful churches and the new houses. 11. The Messiah of the kingdom raises up the faithful men and the faithful women. 12. The good woman sees the good days of the kingdom of love.

LESSON 7

PREPOSITIONS

24. Lexical Study

ἀνά,   *with acc.*, up, again

ἀντί,   *with gen.*, against, instead of

ἀπό,   *with abl.*, from, away from

διά,   *with abl.*, through or by

       with gen., through

       with acc., because of

ἐκ,   *with abl.*, out of (before a vowel this becomes ἐξ)

εἰς,   *with acc.*, into, unto

ἐν,   *with loc.*, in, on

       with inst., by

ἐπί,   *with gen.*, upon, on (emphasizing contact), at, by

       with loc., upon, on, at, over (emphasizing position)

       with acc., upon, on, to, up to (emphasizing motion or direction)

κατά,   *with abl.*, down from

       with gen., down upon

       with acc., along, according to

μετά,   *with gen.*, with

       with acc., after

παρά,   *with abl.*, from

       with loc., before, by the side of, beside

       with acc., beside, beyond, along

περί,   *with gen.*, about, concerning

       with acc., about, around

πρό,   *with abl.*, before

31

πρός,   *with loc.,* at
         with acc., to, toward, with, at
σύν,   *with inst.,* with, together with
ὑπέρ,   *with abl.,* in behalf of, instead of
         with acc., over, above, beyond
ὑπό,   *with abl.,* by (agency)
         with acc., under

25. Grammatical Study[1]

(1) The above vocabulary lists the true prepositions of *Koine* Greek. There are other particles which partake of the nature of prepositions with an adverbial idea added. These are not true prepositions and will be observed in the study of adverbs.

(2) A preposition is a word which is used to help substantives express their case function. It is so named because its position normally is immediately before the substantive with which it is associated.

(3) Prepositions do not govern cases or "take objects." They help substantives to express their relation to verbs or to other parts of speech. They mark the direction and position of the action expressed by the verb. For instance in the sentence φέρει λίθους εἰς τὸν οἶκον the preposition helps the noun to mark the limit of the action of the verb. The function of the cases is much older than the prepositions. Prepositions were developed to aid in expressing case functions already in use. In languages less inflected than Greek (English, for instance) the prepositions have come to be the main way of indicating case function. In Greek both preposition and inflected ending must be considered. Some of the prepositions are used with a variety of cases.

(4) In the above vocabulary the English equivalents for the Greek prepositions are only representative and suggestive. In the actual translation of the Greek New Testament there will be many other possible English translations of some of the prepositions.

---

[1]For full discussion of the function of prepositions see Dana and Mantey, *A Manual Grammar of the Greek New Testament,* and Robertson, *A Grammar of the Greek New Testament in the Light of Historical Research.*

For correct translation one should observe: (1) the basic meaning of the preposition, (2) the case construction with which it is used, and (3) the particular use in any given context. With this considered a correct translation can be given.

(5) One of the predominant uses of the preposition is its combination with a verb to express emphasis. The meaning of a verb may be altered to many shades by the use of prepositions. For instance βλέπω means "I see" while διαβλέπω means "I see through" and, hence, "I see clearly." Observation at this point will be highly profitable. Usually, though not always, a preposition in compound form is repeated before the noun. Example: ἐκφέρω δῶρα ἐκ τοῦ οἴκου. No examples of this usage will appear in the exercises of this lesson.

(6) Prepositions ending in a vowel (except περί and πρό) drop the vowel when the next word begins with a vowel. Examples: ἀπ' ἀδελφοῦ, δι' ἡμερῶν, ἀπάγω, ἐπ' οἴκου. Note the apostrophe which replaces the last vowel except in compound verb forms such as ἀπὸ ἄγω, which becomes ἀπάγω. This is called *elision*. T and π become θ and φ before rough breathing: ἀνθ' ἁμαρτίας, ἀφ' υἱοῦ.

26. Practical Application

(1) Translate the following sentences:

1. ὁ ἀπόστολος διδάσκει ἐν τῇ ἐκκλησίᾳ. 2. ὁ μαθητὴς λέγει παραβολὴν περὶ τῆς βασιλείας. 3. φέρουσιν ἄρτον ἐκ τοῦ οἴκου καὶ πρὸς τοὺς ἀνθρώπους. 4. λαμβάνομεν ἀγαθὰς διδαχὰς ἀπὸ τοῦ πιστοῦ ἀδελφοῦ. 5. οἱ υἱοὶ τοῦ προφήτου λέγουσι λόγους κατὰ τὴν ἀλήθειαν. 6. διὰ τῶν γραφῶν τῶν μαθητῶν γινώσκομεν τὸν νόμον. 7. ὁ ἀδελφὸς πέμπει τοὺς μαθητὰς ἐκ τῶν οἴκων καὶ εἰς τὴν ἐκκλησίαν. 8. ὁ Μεσσίας λέγει παραβολὴν ἐν λόγοις ἀληθείας. 9. ὁ Μεσσίας ἐγείρει τοὺς νεκροὺς ἐκ θανάτου. 10. διὰ τὴν δόξαν τῆς ἐκκλησίας λέγει παραβολὴν ἀγάπης.

(2) Translate the following sentences:

1. The faithful prophets are leading the righteous disciples of the Messiah into the church. 2. After the son the man sees the brother. 3. The man is saying a good word to the disciple and is leading the sons into the house. 4. The apostle is teaching the

men with the sons. 5. We are taking good fruit instead of bad fruit. 6. On account of the good women the prophet is teaching a parable out of the Scriptures. 7. From the temple, through the house, to the church the man leads the sons. 8. After the parable he teaches good things concerning the last days. 9. From the faithful messenger they are hearing words of love. 10. Through the Scriptures we know the teaching. 11. He speaks the truth in love and leads the sons into the kingdom of peace. 12. Through the word of the Messiah the apostles are raising the dead from death.

LESSON 8

PRESENT PASSIVE INDICATIVE

27. Lexical Study

ἀναγινώσκω,	I read	θεός, ὁ,	god, God
βάλλω,	I throw		(usually has
βαπτίζω,	I immerse,		the article when
	I baptize		it means God)
κηρύσσω,	I proclaim,	καρδία, ἡ,	heart
	I preach	κόσμος, ὁ,	world
μένω,	I abide,	ὁδός, ἡ,	road, a way
	I remain	οὐρανός, ὁ,	heaven
σώζω,	I save	τέκνον, τό,	child
ἔρημος, ἡ,	desert	τόπος, ὁ,	place
ζωή, ἡ,	life	φωνή, ἡ,	voice

28. Grammatical Study

(1) The significance of the passive voice is the same in Greek as it is in English — the subject is being acted upon by an outside agent, is receiving the action. Present active λύω, "I am loosing"; present passive λύομαι, "I am being loosed." Thus the present passive pictures continuous action received by the subject in present time.

(2) The primary passive endings are -μαι, -σαι, -ται, -μεθα, -σθε, -νται. These are added to the present stem by means of the variable vowel ο/ε (ο before μ or ν, ε before any other letter). In the development of the language some changes were made. For instance in the second person singular λύεσαι, the σ was lost, the ε and α contracted to η, and the ι became subscript λύῃ.

35

Since this occurs in all verbs of this class, it is wise to learn the short form without indicating all the change.

(3) Present passive indicative of λύω:

Singular	Plural
λύομαι, I am being loosed	λυόμεθα, we are being loosed
λύῃ, you are being loosed	λύεσθε, you are being loosed
λύεται, he (she, it) is being loosed	λύονται, they are being loosed

(4) The student should be able after some drill to form the present passive indicative of all verbs learned up to this point.

(5) There are four distinct uses of the passive voice.

When the *original* (*or direct*) *agent* producing the action on the subject is indicated, the usual construction is ὑπό with the ablative. διδάσκεται ὑπὸ τοῦ ἀγγέλου. "He is being taught by the messenger."

When the agent indicated is the *intermediate* (*or indirect*) *agent* (the medium) through which the original agent acts, the usual construction is διά with the ablative. (Some grammars classify this as a genitive.) ὁ κόσμος ἐγένετο δι᾽ αὐτοῦ. "The world was made through him." Here Christ is looked upon as the intermediate agent of creation; God is the original agent.

When the agent is *impersonal,* the usual construction is the instrumental either with or without the preposition ἐν. οἱ ἄνθρωποι σώζονται ἐν τῷ λόγῳ (or τῷ λόγῳ) τοῦ Μεσσίου. "The men are being saved by the word of the Messiah."

Sometimes the passive is used with *no agent expressed.* Such a use is seen in the expression ἐγείρεται. "He is being raised up."

29. Practical Application

(1) Translate the following sentences.

1. οἱ οἶκοι λύονται ὑπὸ τῶν πονηρῶν ἀνθρώπων. 2. ἡ ἀλήθεια διδάσκεται ἐν τοῖς λόγοις τοῦ ἀποστόλου. 3. ὁ πιστὸς ἀδελφὸς σώζεται ὑπὸ τοῦ μαθητοῦ τοῦ Μεσσίου. 4. ὁ υἱὸς τοῦ Θεοῦ κηρύσσει ἀγάπην καὶ ἀλήθειαν. 5. ζωὴ ἀπὸ τοῦ υἱοῦ μένει ἐν τοῖς δικαίοις ἀνθρώποις. 6. φωνὴ ἀκούεται ἐν τῇ

ἐρήμῳ καὶ ὁδὸς βλέπεται εἰς οὐρανόν. 7. ὁ ἀγαθὸς προφήτης βαπτίζει τὰ τέκνα. 8. ὁ Θεὸς γινώσκει τὰς καρδίας τῶν ἀνθρώπων καὶ πέμπει παραβολὴν ζωῆς. 9. ἀναγινώσκομεν τὴν γραφὴν καὶ γινώσκομεν τὴν ὁδὸν ἀγάπης. 10. οἱ ὄχλοι ἀκούουσι τὰ ἀγαθὰ τῆς βασιλείας τοῦ Θεοῦ καὶ σώζονται ἐκ τοῦ κόσμου.

(2) Translate the following sentences.

1. A parable of the kingdom of heaven is being taught by the faithful apostle. 2. The disciple knows the Son of God and is being saved by the words of truth. 3. The love of God is being preached by the disciples, and they are baptizing the children. 4. The Scripture is being read, and the crowds are being saved from the world. 5. The good women know the life of peace and the way into the kingdom of God. 6. A voice of love, peace, and truth is being raised up at a place in the desert. 7. Hearts are being saved and are abiding in God. 8. Stones are being thrown by evil children into the house of the prophet.

LESSON 9

PRESENT MIDDLE INDICATIVE

30. Lexical Study

αἴρω, I take up, take away   δοξάζω, I glorify
ἀποστέλλω, I send (with a   ἐσθίω, I eat
  message)   κρίνω, I judge
βαίνω, I go   συνάγω, I gather together
  ἀναβαίνω, I go up
  καταβαίνω, I go down

31. Grammatical Study

(1) In the middle voice the subject is acting so as to participate in some way in the results of the action. There is no English equivalent for this Greek construction. The subject rather than the action is the point of emphasis. Special attention is called to the subject.

(2) The following classification of the uses of the middle voice represents the general idea of the construction but admits failure to capture the total force.

The reflexive middle is the one nearest the basic idea. It refers the result of the action directly to the agent. ὁ ἄνθρωπος ἐγείρεται. "The man is raising himself up."

The intensive middle stresses the agent producing the action rather than his participating in the action. διδάσκεται τὴν ἀλήθειαν. "He is teaching the truth." The idea is that "he and no other" is doing the teaching. This corresponds in some ways to the *Piel* stem in Hebrew; it is the "dynamic middle."

The reciprocal middle is the use of a plural subject engaged

38

in an interchange of action. οἱ ἄνθρωποι διδάσκονται. "The men are teaching one another."

(3) The forms of the middle voice in the present, imperfect, and perfect tenses are the same as the passive. The difference is one of function. The context of the passage will indicate whether the construction is middle or passive in function. The present middle indicative of λύω is:

Singular		Plural	
λύομαι,	I loose myself, or I loose for myself	λυόμεθα,	we loose ourselves, etc.
λύῃ,	you loose yourself, etc.	λύεσθε,	you loose yourselves, etc.
λύεται,	he (she, it) looses himself, etc.	λύονται,	they loose themselves, etc.

32. Practical Application

(1) Translate the following sentences:

1. οἱ ἄνθρωποι λαμβάνονται ἄρτον καὶ καρπόν. 2. οἱ μαθηταὶ διδάσκονται τὸν λόγον τῆς ἀληθείας. 3. κρίνεται ἐν τῇ παραβολῇ τοῦ προφήτου. 4. ὁ Μεσσίας συνάγεται τοὺς ὄχλους εἰς τὴν βασιλείαν. 5. οἱ πιστοὶ ἀδελφοὶ ἀναβαίνουσι πρὸς τὸ ἱερὸν σὺν τοῖς υἱοῖς τῶν προφητῶν. 6. ὁ ἄγγελος ἀποστέλλεται ὑπὸ τοῦ Θεοῦ ἐκ τοῦ οἴκου καὶ εἰς τὴν ἔρημον. 7. αἴρουσι λίθους καὶ βάλλουσι τοὺς ἀποστόλους ἐκ τοῦ ἱεροῦ εἰς τὴν ὁδόν. 8. ἡ φωνὴ τοῦ προφήτου ἀκούεται καὶ πονηροὶ ἄνθρωποι βαίνουσι ἐκ τῆς κακῆς ὁδοῦ εἰς τὴν ὁδὸν ἀγάπης καὶ εἰρήνης. 9. οἱ ὄχλοι ἐσθίουσιν ἄρτον καὶ ὁ Μεσσίας δοξάζεται. 10. ἄνθρωποι τοῦ κόσμου δοξάζονται· δίκαιοι ἄνθρωποι δοξάζουσι τὸν Θεόν. 11. ἀγαθοὶ ἄνθρωποι διδάσκονται τοὺς νόμους καὶ τὰς ἐντολὰς τοῦ Θεοῦ. 12. οἱ ἄγγελοι ἀποστέλλονται πρὸς τοὺς υἱοὺς ἀνθρώπων ἐν ταῖς ἐκκλησίαις. 13. ὁ Θεὸς ἀποστέλλει τὸν Μεσσίαν εἰς τὸν κόσμον καὶ ὁ Μεσσίας πέμπει δῶρα τῆς ἀγάπης τοῖς μαθηταῖς. 14. αἱ γραφαὶ ἀναγινώσκονται, ἄνθρωποι σώζονται, καὶ οἱ νεκροὶ ἐγείρονται.

(2) Translate the following sentences:

1. The word of truth is being heard in the world. 2. The sons of the kingdom are judging one another by the parable of the

39

Messiah. 3. God himself sends apostles into the way of evil men. 4. He is taking for himself gifts of bread and fruit. 5. The truth is being taught by the faithful disciples. 6. They go down from the houses, they go up to the church, and they glorify God. 7. The brothers are sending gifts to one another and eating bread in peace. 8. The men of the world are gathering themselves in bad places and are saying to one another evil words.

LESSON 10

PERSONAL PRONOUNS

PRESENT INDICATIVE OF εἰμί. ENCLITICS

33. Lexical Study

ἐγώ, I
σύ, you (sing.)
αὐτός, ή, ό, he, she, it

εἰμί, I am
δέ, but, and, moreover
οὐ, (οὐκ before vowel with
smooth breathing
οὐχ before vowel with
rough breathing), not

34. Grammatical Study

(1) δέ is postpositive, i.e., it cannot stand first in its sentence or clause. Its normal position is second place, although sometimes it appears in third place. ὁ ἀπόστολος ἀναβαίνει πρὸς τὴν ἐκκλησίαν, ὁ δὲ μαθητὴς καταβαίνει πρὸς τὸν οἶκον.

(2) In Greek the negative particle is usually placed immediately in front of the word it negates; hence, its normal position is in front of the verb. ὁ ἀπόστολος οὐκ ἀναβαίνει πρὸς τὴν ἐκκλησίαν.

(3) Declension of personal pronouns.
The personal pronoun of the first person is declined as follows:

Singular		Plural	
N. ἐγώ, I		N. ἡμεῖς, we	
G. ἐμοῦ or μου, of me		G. ἡμῶν, of us	
A. ἐμοῦ or μου, from me		A. ἡμῶν, from us	
D. ἐμοί or μοι, to me		D. ἡμῖν, to us	

41

L. ἐμοί or μοι, in me
I. ἐμοί or μοι, by me
A. ἐμέ or με, —me

L. ἡμῖν, in us
I. ἡμῖν, by us
A. ἡμᾶς, —us

Note the alternative forms μου, μοι, and με. These are the unemphatic forms and are enclitic. The forms ἐμοῦ, ἐμοί, and ἐμέ are the forms to be used when emphasis is desired.

The personal pronoun of the second person is declined as follows:

Singular	Plural
N. σύ, you	ὑμεῖς, you
G. σοῦ or σου, of you	ὑμῶν, of you
A. σοῦ or σου, from you	ὑμῶν, from you
D. σοί or σοι, to you	ὑμῖν, to you
L. σοί or σοι, in you	ὑμῖν, in you
I. σοί or σοι, by you	ὑμῖν, by you
A. σέ or σε, —you	ὑμᾶς, —you

Note the alternative forms σου, σοι, σε which are enclitics and used except where emphasis is desired and the accented forms are used.

The personal pronoun of the third person is declined as follows:

Singular

Masculine	Feminine	Neuter
N. αὐτός, he	αὐτή, she	αὐτό, it
G. αὐτοῦ, of him	αὐτῆς, of her	αὐτοῦ, of it
A. αὐτοῦ, from him	αὐτῆς, from her	αὐτοῦ, from it
D. αὐτῷ, to him	αὐτῇ, to her	αὐτῷ, to it
L. αὐτῷ, in him	αὐτῇ, in her	αὐτῷ, in it
I. αὐτῷ, by him	αὐτῇ, by her	αὐτῷ, by it
A. αὐτόν, — him	αὐτήν, — her	αὐτό, —it

Plural

Masculine	Feminine	Neuter
N. αὐτοί, they	αὐταί, they	αὐτά, they
G. αὐτῶν, of them	αὐτῶν, of them	αὐτῶν, of them

A.	αὐτῶν, from them	αὐτῶν, from them	αὐτῶν, from them
D.	αὐτοῖς, to them	αὐταῖς, to them	αὐτοῖς, to them
L.	αὐτοῖς, in them	αὐταῖς, in them	αὐτοῖς, in them
I.	αὐτοῖς, by them	αὐταῖς, by them	αὐτοῖς, by them
A.	αὐτούς, — them	αὐτάς, — them	αὐτά, — them

(4) The use of personal pronouns in Greek is very similar to the English. They are used to take the place of nouns and avoid monotony. βλέπω τὸν μαθητὴν καὶ διδάσκω τὸν μαθητήν is much better stated βλέπω τὸν μαθητὴν καὶ διδάσκω αὐτόν. The noun for which a pronoun stands is called the antecedent. A pronoun agrees with the antecedent in gender and number; its case is determined by its use in the sentence. Care should be exercised at this point. For example, in the sentence "I have a church and remain in it," "church" is the antecedent of "it." This means that "it" must agree in gender and number with church. The Greek form must be *feminine* to agree with church and not neuter as the English sounds — ἔχω ἐκκλησίαν καὶ μένω ἐν αὐτῇ.

The personal pronouns are not used in the nominative as subjects of verbs unless there is emphasis placed upon them. They are not needed because the subject is cared for in the personal ending of the verb. Emphasis is usually called out in contrast. Thus in the sentence "I am speaking, but you are writing" it would be correct to express the pronoun subject — ἐγὼ λέγω, σὺ δὲ γράφεις.

αὐτός is seldom used in the nominative case. Its use in the nominative case is distinct from its function as a personal pronoun. When used in the *attributive* position whether in the nominative or otherwise, it is to be translated "same." Thus ὁ αὐτὸς ἀπόστολος or ὁ ἀπόστολος ὁ αὐτός will be translated "the same apostle." When it is used in the *predicate* position, it is intensive and should be translated "himself." Thus αὐτὸς ὁ ἀπόστολος, or ὁ ἀπόστολος αὐτός would be translated "the apostle himself." In its intensive form it is often found with pronouns or with the unexpressed subject of a verb. Examples: αὐτὸς ἐγὼ λέγω, or αὐτὸς λέγω would be translated "I myself say." αὐτὸς σὺ λέγεις, or αὐτὸς λέγεις would be translated "you yourself say," etc.

The unemphatic (enclitic) forms of the personal pronoun are

used in the genitive case to express possession. The expression "my word" should be changed to "the word of me" and then translated into Greek ὁ λόγος μου. If emphasis on the possessive idea is required, the "possessive adjective," which will be learned later, is the correct form.

After prepositions the emphatic forms of the personal pronouns are ordinarily used. ἐξ ἐμοῦ rather than ἐκ μου, απ' ἐμοῦ rather than ἀπό μου, etc. However, the form πρός με is frequently found in the New Testament.

(5) Present indicative of εἰμί

Singular		Plural	
εἰμί,	I am	ἐσμέν,	we are
εἶ,	you are	ἐστέ,	you are
ἐστί (ν),	he (she, it) is	εἰσί (ν),	they are

Note: 1. All these forms are enclitic except εἶ.
2. This verb does not have voice. It is a verb showing state of being, not action.
3. ἐστί and εἰσί take movable ν.
4. This verb requires a complement rather than an object, to complete its meaning. ὁ ἄνθρωπός ἐστιν ἀπόστολος. This is an example of the predicate nominative, i.e., the predicate complement in the nominative case.

(6) Enclitics

Enclitics are Greek words which normally have no accent of their own and are pronounced with the word preceding them. The enclitics in this lesson are μου, μοι, με, σου, σοι, σε, and the forms of the present indicative of εἰμί except εἶ. These words tend to throw their accent forward to the word preceding them. For purposes of accenting, enclitics which consist of long syllables are considered short when added to the preceding word. Example: ὁ λόγος μου. For accenting and pronouncing, this construction would be looked upon as a four-syllable word ὁλόγοσμου. The long ultima μου does not prevent an acute on the antepenult in such a construction.

44

The following principles of accent for enclitics should be kept in mind:

1. An enclitic at the beginning of a sentence retains its accent. ἐσμὲν ἄνθρωποι.

2. An enclitic or proclitic is accented before another enclitic. εἴς με, or ὁ ἀδελφός μού ἐστιν ἀγαθός.

3. An acute accent on the ultima is retained in a word standing before any enclitic. It does not change to grave. ὁ Θεός ἐστιν ἀγαθός, or ἀδελφός μου.

4. If a word preceding an enclitic has an acute on the antepenult or a circumflex on the penult, it takes an additional acute on the ultima. ἄνθρωπός ἐστιν, or ὁ οἶκός μου.

5. If the word preceding an enclitic has an acute on the penult or a circumflex or acute on the ultima, an enclitic of one syllable loses its accent. ὁ λόγος μου. ὁ Θεός μου. τοῦ Θεοῦ μου.

6. If a word preceding an enclitic has an acute on the penult or a circumflex on the ultima, an enclitic of two syllables retains its accent. ὁ λόγος ἐστὶν ἀγαθός. ὁ λόγος τοῦ Θεοῦ ἐστὶν ἀγαθός.

35. Practical Application

(1) Translate the following sentences:

1. οἱ μαθηταί σου γινώσκουσι τὴν ἐκκλησίαν καὶ ἄγουσι τοὺς ἀδελφοὺς αὐτῶν εἰς αὐτήν. 2. διδάσκω τοὺς υἱούς μου καὶ λέγω αὐτοῖς παραβολήν. 3. διὰ σοῦ ὁ Θεὸς ἄγει τὰ τέκνα εἰς τὴν βασιλείαν αὐτοῦ καὶ δι᾽ αὐτῶν τοὺς ἄλλους. 4. ἐγώ εἰμι δοῦλος, σὺ δὲ εἶ ἀπόστολος. 5. ἐστὲ προφῆται τοῦ Θεοῦ καὶ ἄγγελοι ἀγάπης. 6. ὁ ἀπόστολος πιστός ἐστιν, οἱ δὲ δοῦλοι αὐτοῦ εἰσὶ πονηροί. 7. οἱ ἀδελφοὶ ἡμῶν βλέπουσιν ἡμᾶς καὶ ἡμεῖς διδάσκομεν αὐτούς. 8. γινώσκομεν τὴν ὁδόν, καὶ δι᾽ αὐτῆς ἄγομεν ὑμᾶς εἰς τὸν οἶκον ἡμῶν.

(2) Translate the following sentences:

1. My brothers are in the church of God. 2. We are saying a parable to you, but you are saying other things to us. 3. The Messiah's disciples are leading their children into his kingdom. 4. My commandment is righteous and my laws are good. 5. Your house is bad, and I am leading my children from it. 6. I am a son, but you are a servant. 7. The disciple himself is saying a

45

parable to the crowd. 8. The same disciple is being heard by the sons of men. 9. I myself am leading my sons to God. 10. The man is good, and I am teaching him the way to my house. 11. He himself is bearing my gifts and his gifts to the temple. 12. God knows his sons and is leading them out of the world into the church.

LESSON 11

DEMONSTRATIVE PRONOUNS

36. Lexical Study

ἁμαρτάνω, I sin
ἁμαρτία, ἡ, sin
ἁμαρτωλός, ὁ, sinner
γάρ, (postpositive),
  for
διδάσκαλος, ὁ, teacher
ἐκεῖνος, η, ο, that
ἐπαγγελία, ἡ, promise

εὐαγγέλιον, τό, gospel, good
  news
κύριος, ὁ, lord, the Lord
λαός, ὁ, people
ὅτι, because, that
οὗτος, αὕτη, τοῦτο, this
χαρά, ἡ, joy
Χριστός, ὁ, Christ

37. Grammatical Study

(1) There are two demonstrative pronouns in Greek. The *near* demonstrative (οὗτος) points out something near at hand; the *remote* demonstrative points out something further removed (ἐκεῖνος).

They are frequently used by themselves with the force of a substantive. οὗτος βλέπει τὸν οἶκον. "This man sees the house." ἐκεῖνος γινώσκει τὸν ἀπόστολον. "That man knows the apostle." In this way αὕτη could mean "this woman" and ἐκείνη could mean "that woman"; οὗτοι, "these men"; ἐκεῖνοι, "those men"; τοῦτο, "this thing," etc.

They are most frequently used with nouns with force similar to that of an adjective. In this use the noun has the article and the demonstrative pronoun stands in the *predicate* position, not the attributive. οὗτος ὁ ἄνθρωπος or ὁ ἄνθρωπος οὗτος would be translated "this man." The same position could be used with either

47

of the demonstratives in any case function. βλέπω ἐκείνην τὴν ἐκκλησίαν. "I see that church," etc.

(2) The demonstratives are declined like the adjectives which follow the first and second declensions. It should be noted that the neuter singular nominative and accusative drop the ν ending.

	Singular			Plural		
	M.	F.	N.	M.	F.	N.
N.	ἐκεῖνος	ἐκείνη	ἐκεῖνο	ἐκεῖνοι	ἐκεῖναι	ἐκεῖνα
G. & A.	ἐκείνου	ἐκείνης	ἐκείνου	ἐκείνων	ἐκείνων	ἐκείνων
D., L., & I.	ἐκείνῳ	ἐκείνῃ	ἐκείνῳ	ἐκείνοις	ἐκείναις	ἐκείνοις
A.	ἐκεῖνον	ἐκείνην	ἐκεῖνο	ἐκείνους	ἐκείνας	ἐκεῖνα

The stem of οὗτος experiences some changes as well as the ending. Observe in the paradigm below that when the ultima has an o-sound vowel, the stem vowel will be ου diphthong; when the ultima has another sound vowel (α or η), the stem vowel will be αυ diphthong.

	Singular			Plural		
	M.	F.	N.	M.	F.	N.
N.	οὗτος	αὕτη	τοῦτο	οὗτοι	αὗται	ταῦτα
G. & A.	τούτου	ταύτης	τούτου	τούτων	τούτων	τούτων
D., L., & I.	τούτῳ	ταύτῃ	τούτῳ	τούτοις	ταύταις	τούτοις
A.	τοῦτον	ταύτην	τοῦτο	τούτους	ταύτας	ταῦτα

38. Practical Application

(1) Translate the following sentences:

1. οὗτος ὁ ἄνθρωπος γινώσκει ἐκεῖνον τὸν ἄνθρωπον. 2. ὁ ἁμαρτωλὸς ἔχει ἁμαρτίαν ἐν τῇ καρδίᾳ αὐτοῦ καὶ οὐ γινώσκει χαράν. 3. ἀκούομεν ταύτην τὴν παραβολὴν περὶ τῆς ἐκκλησίας. 4. εἰς τὴν αὐτὴν ἐκκλησίαν ἄγομεν τούτους τοὺς ἁμαρτωλοὺς καὶ ἐκεῖνα τὰ τέκνα. 5. αὕτη ἀκούει τὴν ἐπαγγελίαν τοῦ Κυρίου αὐτῆς καὶ λέγει τὸ εὐαγγέλιον τῷ λαῷ. 6. οὗτός ἐστιν ἄνθρωπος τοῦ κόσμου, ἐκεῖνος δέ ἐστιν ἄνθρωπος τῆς βασιλείας τοῦ Χριστοῦ. 7. ὁ Κύριος αὐτὸς λέγει λόγους χαρᾶς καὶ ἐγὼ αὐτὸς λαμβάνω τούτους εἰς τὴν καρδίαν

μου. 8. ἐκεῖνοι οἱ ἄγγελοί εἰσιν μαθηταὶ τοῦ αὐτοῦ διδασκάλου καὶ κηρύσσουσι ταύτας τὰς παραβολὰς περὶ ἁμαρτίας καὶ ἁμαρτωλῶν. 9. οὗτος διδάσκει τοὺς ἀγαθοὺς καὶ αὐτὸς διδάσκεται ὑπὸ τοῦ Κυρίου. 10. Χριστός ἐστιν Κύριος τοῦ κόσμου καὶ φέρει ἀγάπην καὶ εἰρήνην καὶ χαρὰν πρὸς αὐτόν.

(2) Translate the following sentences:

1. Through the gospel we have life and joy. 2. The apostle himself baptizes his children and leads them into the church. 3. We ourselves have these sins in our hearts. 4. They are evil sinners, but the Lord leads them from their sin into his kingdom. 5. You are sinning, and because of your sins, you do not have life and joy in you. 6. We know the truth, for we are hearing it from these messengers of the Lord. 7. He himself is going up to the temple because he has sin in his heart. 8. This same Christ is the Messiah of the people and the Lord of the kingdom of God. 9. That man knows peace and joy, but this one knows sin because he is not hearing the promise of God. 10. He himself is a teacher of sinners.

LESSON 12

DEPONENT VERBS. PRESENT INFINITIVES

39. Lexical Study

ἀλλά, but (stronger than δέ)
ἀποκρίνομαι, I answer (*takes dat. case*)
ἄρχω, I rule (*takes gen. case*)
ἄρχομαι, I begin
γίνομαι, I become (*takes complement*)
πορεύομαι, I go

ἔρχομαι, I come or I go
διέρχομαι, I come through
εἰσέρχομαι, I come into, I enter
ἐξέρχομαι, I come out of
κατέρχομαι, I come down
συνέρχομαι, I come with, or together

40. Grammatical Study

(1) Deponent verbs are verbs which appear in the middle or passive *form* but are active in *function*. The name applied is from the Latin *deponere* "to lay aside." Somewhere along the way of the development of the language the active forms were dropped out of preference for the middle or passive. Thus while the *form* changed the *function* did not change. λύω means "I loose," λύομαι means "I loose myself"; but ἔρχομαι means simply "I come," γίνομαι means "I become," ἀποκρίνομαι means "I answer," etc. This is a phenomenon of the language which requires careful study to avoid confusion. The forms will be middle or passive, but the *function* will be active.

(2) Compound verbs are verbs which have a preposition added. Usually the meaning of the preposition will determine the significance of the compound expression. Compare the translations of the compound forms of ἔρχομαι in the above vocabu-

50

lary. Sometimes, however, this is not the case. For instance γινώσκω means "I know," and ἀνά means "up" or "again"; but ἀναγινώσκω means "I read," and ἐπιγινώσκω means "I know fully." These changes are to be observed as a part of vocabulary study.

(3) Some verbs take their object in a case other than the accusative. There is a variety of usage at this point. ἀκούω may take its object in the genitive or the accusative. Usually ἀκούω with the genitive means "to hear without understanding," while with the accusative it means "to hear with understanding." This probably explains the difficulty involved in Acts 9:7 and 22:9. The incident is the experience of Paul in seeing the light and hearing the voice on the road to Damascus. Acts 9:7 states that Paul's companions heard the voice (ἀκούω with the genitive); Acts 22:9 says they did not hear the voice (ἀκούω with the accusative). Thus both constructions say the same thing: the companions of Paul did not understand what the voice said to Paul; to them it was unintelligible sound. ἄρχω in the active voice means "I rule" and takes the genitive case, ἄρχω ἀνθρώπων. In the middle (ἄρχομαι) it means "I begin" and is usually followed by an infinitive, ἄρχομαι διδάσκειν. "I am beginning to teach." ἀποκρίνομαι takes its object in the dative case, ἀποκρίνομαι τοῖς τέκνοις. "I am answering the children." This is sometimes called the dative of the direct object. These are representative cases of verbs which naturally take some case other than the accusative. Many others will be observed in the course of study.

(4) Present Infinitives:

The infinitive is a verbal noun. This means that it partakes of the nature of a verb and the nature of a noun in its function. The full usage will be learned later. For the present purpose note its use as it parallels English use.

The present active infinitive ending is -ειν. This form added to the present stem of any regular ω verb will give the correct form. Examples: λύειν, βλέπειν, ἔχειν, γινώσκειν, etc.

The present middle and passive infinitive ending is -εσθαι. Thus the middle and passive infinitives will be λύεσθαι, βλέπεσθαι, γινώσκεσθαι, etc.

51

The present infinitive of εἰμί is εἶναι.

The voice function of infinitives is the same as that of the indicative mood. The active voice indicates the subject as acting; the middle voice indicates the subject as acting in some way so as to participate in the result of the action; the passive voice indicates that the subject is being acted upon. Note this distinction in the following sentences:

ἄρχομαι λύειν τὸν ἄνθρωπον. "I am beginning to loose the man."
ἄρχομαι λύεσθαι. "I am beginning to loose myself."
ἄρχομαι λύεσθαι ὑπὸ τοῦ ἀνθρώπου. "I am beginning to be loosed by the man."

The significance of the action in the present tense can be learned best in contrast with tenses to be studied later.

41. Practical Application

(1) Translate the following sentences:

1. πορεύομαι ἐκ τοῦ οἴκου καὶ εἰς τὴν ἐκκλησίαν. 2. ὁ προφήτης ἐξέρχεται ἐκ τοῦ ἱεροῦ. 3. ὁ ἄνθρωπος γίνεται ἄγγελος τοῦ κυρίου. 4. ὁ Χριστὸς ἀποκρίνεται τοῖς ἁμαρτωλοῖς ἐν τοῖς λόγοις τῆς παραβολῆς. 5. οὗτος εἰσέρχεται εἰς τὴν βασιλείαν, ἐκεῖνος δὲ μένει ἐν τῷ κόσμῳ τῶν πονηρῶν ἀνθρώπων. 6. συνέρχονται ἐν τῷ οἴκῳ τοῦ Θεοῦ ὅτι γινώσκουσι τὴν ὁδὸν ἀγάπης. 7. λύονται οὗτοι οἱ δοῦλοι ὑπὸ τοῦ κυρίου. 8. ἐν τῷ λόγῳ αὐτοῦ γίνεσθε μαθηταί. 9. οἱ ἁμαρτωλοὶ οὐ βαπτίζονται ὑπὸ τοῦ ἀποστόλου, ἀλλὰ πορεύονται ἐκ τοῦ οἴκου αὐτοῦ εἰς τοὺς οἴκους τῆς ἁμαρτίας. 10. ἄρχῃ γινώσκειν τὰ ἀγαθὰ τῆς βασιλείας τοῦ Θεοῦ. 11. κατερχόμεθα ἐκ τῶν τόπων ἁμαρτίας ὅτι ἡ φωνὴ τοῦ κυρίου ἀκούεται. 12. οἱ υἱοὶ γίνονται ἄνθρωποι ὅτι ἐσθίουσι καρπὸν καὶ ἄρτον. 13. οἱ ἀδελφοὶ ἄρχονται συνέρχεσθαι καὶ ὁ μαθητὴς ἄρχεται δοξάζειν τὸν Θεὸν δι' αὐτούς. 14. ἁμαρτωλοὶ γινώσκουσι τὴν ὁδὸν τοῦ Χριστοῦ, ἀλλὰ κατέρχονται εἰς τὰς ὁδοὺς θανάτου.

(2) Translate the following sentences:

1. We know the love of God and are beginning to teach it to the children. 2. He is coming out of the world and entering the kingdom of God. 3. The Lord is answering the sons of the prophet. 4. Because the word of truth is being heard, you are

becoming disciples of Christ. 5. The crowds are beginning to come out of the houses of sin and to go up to the house of God. 6. They know the teaching of the Lord, but their hearts abide in sin. 7. The child is beginning to be a good son. 8. These sinners are entering God's house, but those are going out into the desert. 9. Sin is beginning to be destroyed by the word of God. 10. I am a sinner, but I am being taught by the Lord's faithful apostle. 11. The apostle says that the Lord is good. 12. These sinners know that this road leads to death.

LESSON 13

IMPERFECT ACTIVE INDICATIVE

42. Lexical Study

ἀποθνήσκω,	I die	νῦν,	adv., now
ἀποκτείνω,	I kill	ἔτι,	adv., still, yet
δέχομαι,	I receive	οὐκέτι,	adv., no longer
ἑτοιμάζω,	I prepare	τότε,	adv., then
θεραπεύω,	I heal	σκοτία, ἡ,	darkness
πιστεύω,	I believe	μέν — δέ,	conj., on the one hand – on the other hand[1]

43. Grammatical Study

(1) The following is the imperfect active indicative of λύω:

Singular	Plural
ἔλυον, I was loosing	ἐλύομεν, we were loosing
ἔλυες, you were loosing	ἐλύετε, you were loosing
ἔλυε, he (she, it) was loosing	ἔλυον, they were loosing

(2) The ε at the beginning of the word is called an augment. It indicates that this is a secondary tense, i.e., a tense which expresses *past* time. Verbs beginning with a consonant add the ε for this augment, and it is called "syllabic augment" because it adds a syllable to the word. Verbs beginning with a vowel form a "temporal augment" by lengthening the vowel to the corresponding long vowel. ε lengthens to η, ο lengthens to ω, and α

---

[1] μέν — δέ are used in contrasting statements. Often the μέν should not be translated and δέ should be translated "but."

54

lengthens to η rather than long α. Examples of augment: ἀκούω becomes ἤκουον, ἐγείρω becomes ἤγειρον, etc.

In compound verbs the augment comes after the preposition and before the verb stem. If the preposition ends with a vowel, elision takes place. Examples: ἐκβάλλω becomes ἐξέβαλλον, ἀποκτείνω becomes ἀπέκτεινον, ἀπάγω becomes ἀπῆγον. Note that the accent may stand on the augment but does not go back to the preposition — ἀπῆγον, not ἄπηγον.

(3) The personal endings in the active secondary tenses are -ν, -s, none, -μεν, -τε, -ν (or σαν). The variable vowel is ο before an ending beginning with μ or ν and ε before any other ending. The third person singular often takes the movable ν. The first person singular and the third person plural are identical and must be distinguished by the context.

(4) The imperfect indicative of εἰμί is:

ἤμην, I was	ἦμεν, we were
ἦs, you were	ἦτε, you were
ἦν, he (she, it) was	ἦσαν, they were

(5) The use of the imperfect tense:

The imperfect tense indicates *continuous* action in *past* time. Contrast "I am loosing" (present) with "I was loosing" (imperfect) and the significance is clear.

There are several varieties of expression in the imperfect. Always it represents continuous action in past time, but this may be presented from different points of view or points of emphasis. The following ideas are frequently found:[1]

The *descriptive* imperfect is used to give a vivid representation of what was going on in past time. It draws a picture of the movement of the event. Matthew 3:5-6 give a good illustration of this graphic use. "Then Jerusalem was going out (ἐξεπορεύετο) to him, and they were being baptized (ἐβαπτίζοντο) in the Jordan river." (See middle and passive forms in next lesson.)

The *repeated* or *iterative* imperfect shows action repeated in

---

[1]For full discussion of this function see Dana and Mantey, *op. cit.* and Robertson, *op. cit.*

55

past time. It would be represented by a broken line (----) rather than a continuous line (_____) which would represent the descriptive imperfect. A good illustration is found in Acts 1:7: "They *were asking him*, 'Lord, art thou at this time restoring the kingdom to Israel?' " This could well be translated "They kept on asking him." The context indicates that the same question was asked Jesus frequently by the disciples. See also Luke 14:7.

The *inceptive* imperfect pictures continuous action in past time, but the emphasis is on the *beginning* of the action rather than its progress; an illustration is Matthew 5:2 ἐδίδασκεν, which might well be translated "he began teaching them." It introduces the teaching given in the sermon on the mount. See also Luke 5:3; Mark 5:37; Acts 3:8.

44. Practical Application

(1) Translate the following sentences:

1. τότε ἠκούομεν τῆς φωνῆς αὐτοῦ, νῦν δὲ οὐκέτι ἀκούομεν αὐτῆς. 2. ἐκεῖνοι μὲν οἱ ἁμαρτωλοὶ μένουσιν ἐν τῇ σκοτίᾳ, οὗτοι δὲ εἰσέρχονται εἰς τὴν βασιλείαν τοῦ θεοῦ. 3. ἐν ἐκείναις ταῖς ἡμέραις ὁ Μεσσίας ἐθεράπευε τοὺς ὄχλους καὶ ἔσωζεν αὐτοὺς ἀπὸ τῶν ἁμαρτιῶν αὐτῶν. 4. ἡτοίμαζον τὰς καρδίας αὐτῶν πονηροὶ ἄνθρωποι ὅτι ἤκουον τῶν γραφῶν καὶ ἐπίστευον αὐτάς. 5. διὰ μὲν τήν ἀγάπην τοῦ Θεοῦ ἀποθνήσκομεν ἐν τῇ βασιλείᾳ τοῦ Θεοῦ, δεχόμεθα δὲ τὴν ζωὴν σὺν τῷ υἱῷ αὐτοῦ. 6. πονηροὶ ἦτε, ἀγαθοὶ δέ ἐστε. 7. νῦν μὲν διδασκόμεθα ὑπὸ τοῦ κυρίου, τότε δὲ ἐδιδάσκομεν τὴν ἐκκλησίαν. 8. ὁ Μεσσίας ἀπέστελλεν ἀγγέλους πρὸς ἡμᾶς. 9. οἱ ἄνθρωποι οἱ πονηροὶ ἀπέκτεινον τὰ τέκνα σὺν τοῖς διδασκάλοις αὐτῶν. 10. ἐν τῷ κόσμῳ ἦν καὶ ὁ κόσμος οὐκ ἐγίνωσκεν αὐτόν.

(2) Translate the following sentences:

1. The Lord was still in the temple, but they were not seeing him. 2. On account of the truth of God, you were dying in those evil days. 3. They are still in their sins because they are not coming into the kingdom of God. 4. The evil men were killing the disciples, but the disciples were not dying in darkness and sin. 5. The apostles were preparing their hearts and preaching the gospel to sinners. 6. The same sinners were receiving the gospel of love and peace with joy. 7. Then he was a servant, but now he is a

beloved son. 8. You (pl.) are no longer abiding in the darkness of sin because you hear the voice of the Lord. 9. The sons of the prophets were gathering the good gifts together into the temple. 10. You (sing.) are no longer a sinner because you are believing the gospel of God's love and are being saved by it.

LESSON 14

IMPERFECT MIDDLE AND PASSIVE INDICATIVE

45. Lexical Study

βιβλίον, τό, book
δαιμόνιον, τό, demon
ἔργον, τό, work
θάλασσα, ἡ, sea
πλοῖον, τό, boat

καθαρίζω, I cleanse, I purify
οὐδέ, *conj.*, and not, nor,
    not even
οὐδὲ . . . οὐδέ, neither . . . nor
οὔπω, *adv.*, not yet

Begin with Lesson 2 and form the imperfect indicative first person singular of all verbs up to this lesson. Note: The imperfect of ἔχω is εἶχον, etc.

46. Grammatical Study

(1) The imperfect middle and passive voice forms are identical just as they are in the present tense. The difference is one of function. Note the English translation of the following paradigms.

Imperfect middle indicative of λύω

Singular		Plural	
ἐλυόμην,	I was loosing myself, or for myself	ἐλυόμεθα,	we were loosing ourselves, etc.
ἐλύου,	you were loosing yourself, etc.	ἐλύεσθε,	you were loosing yourselves, etc.
ἐλύετο,	he was loosing himself, etc.	ἐλύοντο,	they were loosing themselves, etc.

58

Imperfect passive indicative of λύω

Singular		Plural	
ἐλυόμην,	I was being loosed	ἐλυόμεθα,	we were being loosed
ἐλύου,	you were being loosed	ἐλύεσθε,	you were being loosed
ἐλύετο,	he (she, it) was being loosed	ἐλύοντο,	they were being loosed

(2) The personal endings of the middle secondary tenses are -μην, -σο, -το, -μεθα, -σθε, -ντο. The variable vowel ο/ε appears here as in the active. The second person singular is altered by the loss of the σ and the contraction of the connecting vowel ε and the ending ο. Thus ἐλύεσο becomes ἐλύου.

Verbs which are deponent in the present are also deponent in the imperfect; hence, there will be no imperfect active forms for such verbs as ἔρχομαι, ἀποκρίνομαι, etc. The imperfect middle *forms* will have imperfect active *function*. I was coming — ἠρχόμην, etc.

(3) It is an idiom of Greek that a neuter plural subject practically always has its verb in the singular. τὰ τέκνα ἔχει (not ἔχουσι) καρπὸν καὶ ἄρτον.

(4) Other uses of καί must be observed. Its basic use is as a simple connective as it has been used up to here. It has, however, other uses. Frequently it is used to mean "also" or "even." When it is used in this way its position in Greek is immediately in front of the word with which it is logically connected. In English usage "also" takes the reverse order from Greek, i.e., it stands after the word with which it is connected. "Even" takes the same order as Greek. The context must determine whether καί is a simple connective, to be translated "even", or additional to be translated "also." γινώσκουσι καὶ ἁμαρτωλοὶ τὸν νόμον. "Even sinners know the law." τοῦτο δὲ καὶ ἐγὼ γινώσκω. "But this I also know." καὶ . . . καὶ is a correlative construction which should be translated "both . . . and." καὶ οἱ μαθηταὶ καὶ οἱ προφῆται γινώσκουσι τοῦτο. "Both the disciples and the prophets know this."

59

(5) οὐδέ is often a *simple* negative connective and is translated "and not" or "nor." οὐ γινώσκω τοῦτο, οὐδὲ γινώσκεις αὐτό. "I do not know this nor do you know it." At other times οὐδέ is used *emphatically* and should be translated "not even." οὐδὲ οἱ προφῆται βλέπουσι τὸν Θεόν. "Not even the prophets see God." Another use of οὐδέ is the *correlative* use in which οὐδέ . . . οὐδέ is to be translated "neither . . . nor." οὐδὲ οἱ μαθηταὶ γινώσκουσι τοῦτο οὐδὲ οἱ προφῆται. "Neither the disciples nor the prophets know this."

47. Practical Application

(1) Translate the following sentences:

1. οὗτοι οἱ λόγοι ἐν τῷ βιβλίῳ ἐγράφοντο. 2. καὶ οἱ λόγοι καὶ αἱ γραφαὶ τῶν προφητῶν ἠκούοντο ὑπὸ τῶν ἁμαρτωλῶν. 3. ἐν ἐκείναις ταῖς ἡμέραις οὐδὲ ἐδιδασκόμεθα ὑπ᾽ αὐτοῦ οὐδὲ ἐδιδάσκομεν τοὺς ἄλλους. 4. τότε ὄχλος ἐξεπορεύετο πρὸς αὐτόν, νῦν δὲ οὐκέτι ἐκπορεύεται. 5. καὶ πρὸς τοὺς πονηροὺς ἀδελφοὺς ἐφέρετο τὰ δῶρα. 6. οὔπω βλέπουσι τὸν κύριον ἐν τῇ δόξῃ αὐτοῦ, ἀλλὰ ἐδιδάσκοντο ὑπ᾽ αὐτοῦ καὶ ἐν ταῖς ἡμέραις ταῖς κακαῖς. 7. οἱ μαθηταὶ κατήρχοντο πρὸς τὴν θάλασσαν καὶ εἰσηρχόμεθα εἰς τὸ πλοῖον σὺν τῷ κυρίῳ. 8. ὁ Μεσσίας ἐξέβαλλε τὰ δαιμόνια ἐκ τῶν ἁμαρτωλῶν καὶ ἐκαθάριζεν αὐτοὺς ἀπὸ τῶν ἁμαρτιῶν αὐτῶν. 9. ἐσμὲν ἐν τῷ κόσμῳ, ἐσμὲν δὲ καὶ ἐν τῇ βασιλείᾳ τοῦ Θεοῦ. 10. διὰ τὸν λόγον τοῦ κυρίου τὰ δαιμόνια ἐξήρχετο ἐκ τῶν ἀνθρώπων.

(2) Translate the following sentences:

1. In behalf of his children these books were being written by him. 2. On account of the word of God the messengers were being received into the houses of the disciples. 3. You were neither receiving the truth from us nor bearing it to others. 4. Both the love and the peace of God are being heard in the church. 5. Not even the good men are being saved by works. 6. They know the books of the men, but they know also the Scriptures of God. 7. Men were being cleansed from their sin by the Messiah and were being saved by his teachings. 8. We were going down to the sea with the apostles and entering a boat with the Lord. 9. You (pl.) were not being killed in behalf of him, but he was dying in behalf of you. 10. The demons were being cast out of the men and their children.

LESSON 15

FUTURE ACTIVE AND MIDDLE INDICATIVE

48. Lexical Study[1]

ἄξω, I shall lead	γενήσομαι, I shall become
ἀκούσω, I shall hear	γνώσομαι, I shall know
βλέψω, I shall see	ἐλεύσομαι, I shall come, go
σώσω, I shall save	λήμψομαι, I shall take

49. Grammatical Study

(1) The future active of λύω is:

λύσω, I shall loose	λύσομεν, we shall loose
λύσεις, you will loose	λύσετε, you will loose
λύσει, he (she, it) will loose	λύσουσι, they will loose

(2) The future middle of λύω is:

λύσομαι, I shall loose myself, or for myself	λυσόμεθα, we shall loose ourselves
λύσῃ, you will loose yourself	λύσεσθε, you will loose yourselves
λύσεται, he will loose himself	λύσονται, they will loose themselves

(3) The *future stem* is obtained by adding a σ to the verb stem. For example, the verb stem of λύω is λυ-. Add σ and the future stem is λυσ-. This is a primary tense; hence, the primary active and primary middle endings are used. They are added to

---

[1]The student should study paragraph 49 of this lesson carefully before he learns this vocabulary.

the future stem by means of the variable vowel (o and ε) just like the present. Thus it is observed that the future active of λύω is exactly like the present active except for the tense suffix σ. The future middle of λύω is exactly like the present middle except for the tense suffix σ. The future passive is built on a different stem entirely from the future middle and should not be confused with it. λύσομαι means "I shall loose myself," but it does *not* mean "I shall be loosed."

Not all future stems are as easily determined as that of λύω. When the verb stem ends in a consonant, there is a basic change when the tense suffix σ is added. The following chart indicates the change which *generally* takes place. This is by no means universal. To be entirely safe the beginner should consult the Greek-English vocabulary in the back of the book to determine the future stem. The *second* form will always be the future indicative first person singular. With this form known, it is easy to form the remainder of the future active or middle.

Stem Changes in Future Stems

Verb stems ending in a liquid consonant (λ, μ, ν, ρ) usually drop the σ and accent the ω. This is due to contraction principles to be learned later. Thus μένσω becomes μενῶ "I shall abide." Sometimes there are other stem changes. For instance, ἀποστέλλω becomes ἀποστελῶ in the future.

Verb stems ending in a mute consonant experience the following changes:
A palatal κ, γ, or χ before σ becomes ξ. ἄγω becomes ἄξω.
A labial π, β, or φ before σ becomes ψ. βλέπω becomes βλέψω.
A dental τ, δ, or θ before σ drops out. πείθω becomes πείσω.

Verbs ending in a sibilant consonant drop the sibilant before the σ of the future. σώζω becomes σώσω.

Some future stems are entirely different from present stems. This is due to the fact that the general verb stem and the present stem are not always the same. In λύω they are the same; hence, the similarity of present and future. The verb stem of γινώσκω, however, is γνω-; the future stem will be γνωσ-. The verb stem of κηρύσσω is κηρυκ-; the future stem will be κηρυξ-. The verb stem of βαπτίζω is βαπτιδ-; the future will be βαπτισ-. This accounts for the great variety of differences between future stem forms. Once the first person singular of the future is learned it is an easy matter to know the remainder of the tense forms.

Some verbs are *active* in the present tense but *deponent* in the future tense. This should be carefully observed in the process of vocabulary study. Examples are λαμβάνω (λήμψομαι) and γινώσκω (γνώσομαι).

(4) The *time* of action of the future tense is obvious. The *kind* of action may be either punctiliar or linear; the context will usually indicate which is intended. Usually it is punctiliar. The most natural construction for indicating continuous action in future time is the periphrastic future which will be studied later.

There is a variety of usage possible with this tense. The simple *predictive future* may be indicated, ὑμᾶς διδάξει. The *imperative* may be expressed by the future. καλέσεις τὸ ὄνομα αὐτοῦ Ἰωάνην. "You shall call his name John." The *deliberative* future is sometimes found when a rhetorical question is being asked, i.e., one which does not really expect an answer. Κύριε, πρὸς τίνα ἀπελευσόμεθα; "Lord, to whom shall we go?" These are examples of frequently found future ideas. Others occur in the New Testament less frequently.

(5) The future indicative of εἰμί is

ἔσομαι, I shall be	ἐσόμεθα, we shall be
ἔσῃ, you will be	ἔσεσθε, you will be
ἔσται, he (she, it) will be	ἔσονται, they will be

50. Practical Application

(1) Translate the following sentences:

1. ὁ Χριστὸς ἄξει τοὺς μαθητὰς αὐτοῦ εἰς τὴν ὁδὸν τῆς ἀγάπης. 2. ἐν ἐκείνῃ τῇ ἡμέρᾳ ὁ Μεσσίας ἐλεύσεται σὺν τοῖς ἀγγέλοις αὐτοῦ. 3. ἁμαρτωλοὶ μέν ἐστε, γενήσεσθε δὲ υἱοὶ τοῦ Θεοῦ. 4. τότε γνώσονται ὅτι αὐτός ἐστιν ὁ Κύριος. 5. λήμψεσθε καὶ τὰ δῶρα καὶ τοὺς οἴκους. 6. οὐδὲ ἐγὼ ταῦτα γνώσομαι. 7. αἱ ἡμέραι αἱ κακαὶ ἐλεύσονται. 8. τὰ τέκνα βλέψει τὸν

ἄγγελον ἐν τῇ ἐκκλησίᾳ. 9. κηρύξουσι τὸ εὐαγγέλιον καὶ δέξονται ἁμαρτωλοὺς μετὰ χαρᾶς. 10. οἱ μαθηταὶ ἀκούσουσι τῆς φωνῆς τοῦ Κυρίου αὐτῶν
καὶ ἄξουσι τὰ τέκνα πρὸς αὐτόν. 11. ἐσόμεθα σὺν αὐτῷ ἐν τῇ βασιλείᾳ
αὐτοῦ. 12. εἶ πονηρός, ἀλλ᾽ ἔσῃ ἀγαθός.

(2) Translate the following sentences:

1. The kingdom of God is in you. 2. You will know the truth of
God in that day. 3. They will lead the sinners and the children
into the same church. 4. Now the world sees evil days, but then it
will see the glory of Christ. 5. No longer will men be in darkness. 6. The gifts were being taken from the children by us, but
we shall no longer take them. 7. The voice of the prophet will
prepare a way in the hearts of men. 8. In those days you were
evil, but now you are hearing the gospel and you will become
good men. 9. In this world we have death, but in heaven we
shall have life with the Son of God. 10. They were teaching
against the Messiah, but now they will teach in behalf of him.
11. Now we are not seeing him, but in that day we shall both
see and know him. 12. These men are not yet good, but on account
of the word of God, they will become good.

LESSON 16

FIRST AORIST ACTIVE AND MIDDLE INDICATIVE

51. Lexical Study[1]

ἤκουσα,	I heard	ἔγραψα,	I wrote
ἔβλεψα,	I saw	ἔπεμψα,	I sent
ἐδίδαξα,	I taught	ἐβάπτισα,	I baptized
ἐθεράπευσα,	I healed	ἔσωσα,	I saved
ἐκήρυξα,	I preached	ἐδόξασα,	I glorified

52. Grammatical Study

(1) The first aorist active indicative of λύω is:

ἔλυσα,	I loosed	ἐλύσαμεν,	we loosed
ἔλυσας,	you loosed	ἐλύσατε,	you loosed
ἔλυσε(ν),	he (she, it) loosed	ἔλυσαν,	they loosed

(2) The first aorist middle indicative of λύω is:

ἐλυσάμην,	I loosed myself, or for myself	ἐλυσάμεθα,	we loosed ourselves, etc.
ἐλύσω,	you loosed yourself, etc.	ἐλύσασθε,	you loosed yourselves, etc.
ἐλύσατο,	he (she, it) loosed himself, etc.	ἐλύσαντο,	they loosed themselves, etc.

(3) In Greek, as in English, there are two ways to form the past tense. This does not mean that each verb has two ways of forming the past tense. Some Greek verbs do but they are rare. In English the verb "preach" forms its past tense by adding "ed":

---

[1]Study paragraph 52 before learning the vocabulary.

"I preach" (present), "I preached" (past). The verb "teach" forms its past tense by a stem change: "I teach" (present), "I taught" (past). So in Greek there are two ways called "first aorist" and "second aorist." Some Greek verbs add a σ to the stem and are called "first aorist"; others add the endings without the σ and are called "second aorist." There is *no difference in function* between the two.

The aorist is a secondary tense, i.e., it deals with action in *past time*. It is, therefore, augmented just as the imperfect tense: a stem beginning with a consonant takes "syllabic augment"; a stem beginning with a vowel takes "temporal augment."

As a secondary tense the aorist takes the secondary active endings in the active and the secondary middle endings in the middle. The aorist passive is entirely different from the middle in form as well as function. To the augmented stem of λύω, ελυ-, add the σ (tense suffix, a few verbs take κ instead of σ), the short a (connecting vowel) and the secondary personal endings. There are minor changes in the inflection of the word in first and third persons singular active and in second person singular middle. The reasons for these changes are not of importance here.

(4) As in the future so in the aorist there are changes which take place when the tense suffix σ is added to the stem of some verbs. In general the changes in the aorist are the same as in the future but this is *not a safe test* for determining the aorist. The beginner should always check the word in the vocabulary in the back of the book to determine what the aorist first person singular is to be; the remaining forms will be easy. The *third* form in the group will be the aorist. Example: λύω, λύσω, ἔλυσα, etc.

(5) The function of the aorist tense is a matter of tremendous importance. The *time* of action is past. The *kind* of action is punctiliar. Thus is observed the difference between the imperfect and the aorist. The imperfect indicates continuous action in past time — ἔλυον "I was loosing"; the aorist indicates finished action in past time — ἔλυσα "I loosed." The imperfect is a "moving picture"; the aorist is a "snapshot." The Greek aorist may be translated by either the simple past tense in English "I loosed"

66

or the perfect tense in English "I have loosed." Usually the context will indicate which is to be used. There are several shades of meaning in the use of the aorist tense. The major ones are the *constative* in which the action is looked upon in its entirety — ἐβάπτισε τοὺς ἀνθρώπους. Actually the act may have covered considerable time but it is presented as *one* act. The *ingressive* aorist views the act as having occurred but emphasizes the initiation: δι' ὑμᾶς ἐπτώχευσε. "For your sakes he became poor." The act is one but viewed from its initiation. The *culminative* aorist views the act as having occurred but emphasizes the end of the action or the state of being resulting from the action. At this point the aorist encroaches upon the function of the Greek perfect, which will be studied later. τὸν πρῶτον λόγον ἐποιησάμην. "The former treatise I have made." The act of writing is looked upon as one act but the emphasis is on the finished product. Other less frequently found constructions are treated at length in Dana and Mantey, and in Robertson.

53. Practical Application

(1) Translate the following sentences:

1. ἔλυσεν ὁ κύριος τοὺς δούλους αὐτοῦ. 2. ἐπέμψαμεν τὰ τέκνα ἐκ τοῦ οἴκου. 3. οἱ μαθηταὶ ἐδόξασαν τὸν Θεὸν καὶ τὸν υἱὸν αὐτοῦ. 4. διὰ τοὺς λόγους ὑμῶν ἐβλέψαμεν τὴν πονηρὰν ὁδὸν τοῦ κόσμου. 5. ἐκήρυξας τὸ εὐαγγέλιον καὶ οἱ ἀδελφοί σου ἤκουσαν αὐτὸ καὶ ἐπίστευσαν. 6. ἔγραψε παραβολὴν καὶ ἔπεμψεν αὐτὴν πρὸς τὴν ἐκκλησίαν. 7. ὁ Μεσσίας ἐδίδαξεν ἐν τῷ ἱερῷ καὶ ἐν τῷ οἴκῳ. 8. ἡτοίμασε τοῖς μαθηταῖς τόπον ἐν τῷ οὐρανῷ. 9. ἔσωσα ὑμᾶς ἐγώ, ὑμεῖς δὲ οὐκ ἐδέξασθε ἐμὲ εἰς τοὺς οἴκους ὑμῶν. 10. ἠκούσατε ἐκείνας τὰς ἐντολὰς ἐν τῷ ἱερῷ, ἄλλας δὲ ἐν τῇ ἐκκλησίᾳ ἀκούσετε.

(2) Translate the following sentences:

1. They heard his voice but did not receive his words. 2. The evil men saw the Lord, and he preached to them the way of life. 3. The servants have prepared gifts and houses for the disciples. 4. Even those evil men glorified God on account of your words. 5. We have preached the gospel to them and have baptized their

children. 6. The Lord of life healed the sinners and saved them. 7. You (pl.) received the same parables and believed the same Christ. 8. He has not sent the books nor will he send them. 9. These good women glorified God because he healed their brothers and saved their sons. 10. You (sing.) began to preach the gospel because you heard the voice of the Lord.

LESSON 17

SECOND AORIST ACTIVE AND MIDDLE INDICATIVE

54. Lexical Study

ἔβαλον,	I threw, cast	λείπω,	I leave
εἶδον,	I saw	ἔλιπον,	I left
εἶπον,	I said	πάσχω,	I suffer
ἔλαβον,	I took	ἔπαθον,	I suffered
ἤγαγον,	I led	πίπτω,	I fall
ἦλθον,	I came, went	ἔπεσον,	I fell
ἤνεγκα,	(1st aor.)	ἔσχον,	I had
ἤνεγκον,	(2nd aor.), I bore, brought	ἔφαγον,	I ate

55. Grammatical Study

(1) The second aorist active indicative of λείπω is:

ἔλιπον,	I left	ἐλίπομεν,	we left
ἔλιπες,	you left	ἐλίπετε,	you left
ἔλιπε(ν),	he (she, it) left	ἔλιπον,	they left

(2) The second aorist middle indicative of λείπω is:

ἐλιπόμην,	I left for myself	ἐλιπόμεθα,	we left for ourselves
ἐλίπου,	you left for yourself	ἐλίπεσθε,	you left for yourselves
ἐλίπετο,	he left for himself	ἐλίποντο,	they left for themselves

(3) The form of the second aorist was introduced in the last lesson. This is the past tense of verbs which do not add σ to

69

the stem but alter the stem radically and add the regular secondary personal endings active and middle. As in the first aorist the aorist passive is altogether different from the aorist middle. There is no way to determine whether a Greek verb will take first or second aorist. This must be determined by reference to the vocabulary in the back of the book. Once this is determined the forms will be readily known. There are a few irregular second aorists, but for the most part they are regularly formed.

Find the stem by striking off the -ον of the first person singular and the augment if it is syllabic; if it is temporal, it must be shortened back to its original vowel. Thus the stem of ἔλιπον is λιπ-, of ἔλαβον it is λαβ-, and of ἦλθον it is ἐλθ-, etc. To the augmented stem add the secondary active or the secondary middle endings by using the connecting vowel ο/ε.

Note that the only form difference between the imperfect and the second aorist is that the imperfect is formed on the present stem ἔλειπον, "I was leaving," and the second aorist is formed on the aorist stem ἔλιπον, "I left."

(4) The function of the second aorist is exactly the same as that of the first aorist. The difference is one of form only. Hence the first aorist ἤνεγκα and the second aorist ἤνεγκον of φέρω mean the same "I bore" or "I brought." Verbs that have both aorist forms are rare.

(5) The second aorist εἶδον is really from the verb εἴδω though some grammars classify it as a second aorist of βλέπω. The second aorist εἶπον is really from the verb φημί though it is sometimes classified as a second aorist of λέγω. This verb, when used in the New Testament, frequently has first aorist endings on the second aorist stem. The same is true of εἶδον. It should be noted that ἔρχομαι, which is deponent in the present system, has active forms in the aorist system — ἦλθον not ἠλθόμην. This is true of all its compound derivatives.

56. Practical Application

(1) Translate the following sentences:

1. παρέλαβε τὴν ἐπαγγελίαν παρὰ τοῦ Μεσσίου, καὶ κηρύσσει αὐτὴν ἐν

70

τῇ ἐκκλησίᾳ. 2. ἐγένοντο οἱ μαθηταὶ τοῦ Κυρίου. 3. ὁ Χριστὸς ἐξέβαλε τὰς ἁμαρτίας τῶν ἁμαρτωλῶν καὶ ἐθεράπευσεν αὐτούς. 4. καὶ εἴδομεν τὸν Κύριον καὶ ἠκούσαμεν τῶν λόγων αὐτοῦ. 5. οἱ ἀπόστολοι εἶδον τὸν υἱὸν τοῦ Θεοῦ, ἐγένετο γὰρ αὐτὸς ἄνθρωπος καὶ ἔμενεν ἐν τῷ κόσμῳ. 6. ταῦτα εἴπετε ἡμῖν ἐν τῷ ἱερῷ, ἐκεῖνα δὲ ἐν τῷ οἴκῳ. 7. οὐδὲ εἰσῆλθες εἰς τὴν ἐκκλησίαν, οὐδὲ εἶπες λόγους ἀγάπης τοῖς τέκνοις. 8. τὰ ἱερὰ αἱ πισταὶ ἔλιπον, καὶ κατῆλθον εἰς τοὺς οἴκους αὐτῶν. 9. ὁ ἄνθρωπος ἤγαγε τὰ τέκνα πρὸς τὸν Κύριον ὅτι ἔσχε τὴν ἀγάπην τοῦ Θεοῦ ἐν τῇ καρδίᾳ αὐτοῦ. 10. οἱ δίκαιοι ἔφαγον ἄρτον ἐν τῇ ἐρήμῳ καὶ ἐδόξασαν τὸν Θεόν. 11. ὁ Χριστὸς ἔπαθε πονηρὰ ὑπὲρ ἁμαρτωλῶν. 12. τὰ τέκνα ἤνεγκε λίθους καὶ εἰσέβαλεν αὐτοὺς εἰς τὸν οἶκον τοῦ προφήτου.

(2) Translate the following sentences:

1. The sinners ate the Lord's bread, but they did not glorify God. 2. Stones fell from the house, and the children bore them into the desert. 3. The Son of God suffered in those days. 4. You left your brother in the house of sin, but I am leading him to the Lord. 5. The sinners had houses, but they left them because the voice of the Messiah was being heard in the church. 6. We saw the Lord, we heard his parables, and we became his disciples. 7. The children said bad words because they heard them from the evil men. 8. He took gifts of bread, but I took gifts of fruit. 9. The brothers say that they saw the Lord and heard parables from him. 10. You have become righteous because the Son of God came down from heaven and into your hearts.

LESSON 18

AORIST PASSIVE INDICATIVE AND FUTURE PASSIVE INDICATIVE

57. Lexical Study

ἐβλήθην,	I was thrown	ἐπορεύθην,	I went
ἐγενήθην,	I became	ἠκούσθην,	I was heard
ἐγνώσθην,	I was known	ἐλείφθην,	I was left
ἐδιδάχθην,	I was taught	ἀπεστάλην,	I was sent
ἐκηρύχθην,	I was preached	ἐγράφην,	I was written
ἐλήμφθην,	I was taken	ὤφθην,	I was seen

58. Grammatical Study

(1) The first aorist passive of λύω is:

ἐλύθην, I was loosed	ἐλύθημεν, we were loosed
ἐλύθης, you were loosed	ἐλύθητε, you were loosed
ἐλύθη, he (she, it) was loosed	ἐλύθησαν, they were loosed

The first aorist passive has as a tense suffix the syllable θε which in the indicative appears as θη. As a secondary tense the aorist passive is augmented in the regular way and takes secondary personal endings added without the use of a connecting vowel. It should be noted that the secondary *active* endings are used even though this is passive in voice. The first aorist passive of λύω will then be ἐλύθην, etc.

When the verb stem ends with a consonant there are various changes before the θη of the aorist passive. In general these are

72

the changes made; always check the vocabulary in the back of the book until you learn the aorist passive form:

Liquid consonants:

ν drops out before θ. κρίνω, ἐκρίθην.
λ, ρ are retained before θ. ἀγγέλλω, ἠγγέλθην. αἴρω, ἤρθην.
μ inserts η before θ. νέμω, ἐνεμήθην.

Mute consonants:

1. Palatals:
   κ, γ change to χ before θ. ἄγω, ἤχθην. διώκω, ἐδιώχθην.
   χ is retained before θ. διδάσκω (διδαχ-), ἐδιδάχθην.

2. Labials:
   π, β change to φ before θ. λείπω, ἐλείφθην. τρίβω, ἐτρίφθην.
   φ elides the θ and becomes second aorist. See next paragraph.

3. Dentals:
   τ, δ, θ change to σ before θ. πείθω, ἐπείσθην, etc.

4. Sibilants change to σ before θ. βαπτίζω, ἐβαπτίσθην, etc.

(2) The second aorist passive of ἀποστέλλω is:

ἀπεστάλην, I was sent   ἀπεστάλημεν, we were sent
ἀπεστάλης, you were sent   ἀπεστάλητε, you were sent
ἀπεστάλη, he (she, it) was sent   ἀπεστάλησαν, they were sent

The second aorist passive is like the first aorist passive except for the absence of the θ. Check the difference in the paradigm above and in γράφω which becomes in the aorist passive ἐγράφην, ἐγράφης, ἐγράφη, etc. The aorist passive of a verb cannot be determined by the aorist active. Some verbs have first aorist active and second aorist passive (γράφω). Others have second aorist active and first aorist passive (λείπω).

As to function, the two are the same. They indicate finished action received by the subject in past time. Compare λύομαι, "I am being loosed"; ἐλυόμην, "I was being loosed"; and ἐλύθην, "I was loosed."

73

(3) The future passive of λύω is:

λυθήσομαι, I shall be loosed λυθησόμεθα, we shall be loosed
λυθήσῃ, you will be loosed λυθήσεσθε, you will be loosed
λυθήσεται, he (she, it) will λυθήσονται, they will be loosed
be loosed

The future passive indicative is based on the aorist passive stem. As a primary tense it has no augment and uses the primary passive personal endings. In addition to this it has the future tense suffix σ and the variable connecting vowel ο/ε. Note these component parts in the form λυθή-σ-ο-μαι, "I shall be loosed."

In function the future passive deals with action received by the subject in future time. Generally the kind of action is punctiliar. It may be linear as in the future active. The context is the best test for determining the kind of action.

(4) Deponent verbs vary in the aorist and future passive. Some have passive forms. Of this group ἀποκρίνομαι is an example; the deponent form for aorist passive is ἀπεκρίθην, "I answered."

Some deponent verbs have both passive and middle forms in the aorist. γίνομαι, "I become" sometimes appears ἐγενόμην and sometimes ἐγενήθην. Both forms should be translated, "I became"; there is no difference in function.

59. Practical Application

(1) Translate the following sentences:

1. ἐδιδάχθητε ὑπὸ τῶν ἀποστόλων τοῦ Κυρίου. 2. ἐν ἐκείνῃ τῇ ἡμέρᾳ οἱ νεκροὶ ἐγερθήσονται ἐν τῷ λόγῳ τοῦ Θεοῦ. 3. ταῦτα ἐγράφη ἐν ταῖς γραφαῖς. 4. οὗτοι οἱ ἁμαρτωλοὶ συνήχθησαν εἰς τὸν οἶκον τοῦ προφήτου. 5. νῦν μὲν πέμπονται οἱ μαθηταί, τότε δὲ ἐπέμφθησαν καὶ οἱ ἀπόστολοι καὶ οἱ ἄγγελοι. 6. διὰ τῆς ἀγάπης τοῦ Χριστοῦ οἱ ἁμαρτωλοὶ ἐσώθησαν καὶ ἐγενήθησαν μαθηταὶ τοῦ Κυρίου. 7. ἐπορεύθημεν εἰς ἕτερον τόπον, ἐκεῖνοι γὰρ οὐκ ἐδέξαντο ἡμᾶς. 8. τὸ εὐαγγέλιον ἐκηρύχθη ἐν ἐκείναις ταῖς ἡμέραις, καὶ κηρυχθήσεται καὶ νῦν. 9. ἡ φωνὴ ἠκούσθη καὶ ὁ ἀπόστολος ἀπεστάλη εἰς τὸν κόσμον. 10. τῶν ἁμαρτωλῶν πρῶτός εἰμι, καὶ δὲ ἐγὼ ἐσώθην τῇ ἀγάπῃ τοῦ Θεοῦ. 11. εἰσῆλθες εἰς τὴν ἐκκλησίαν τοῦ Κυρίου καὶ ἐβαπτίσθης. 12. ἐν ἐκείναις ταῖς ἡμέραις ἀκουσθήσεται ὁ λόγος τῆς εἰρήνης.

74

(2) Translate the following sentences:

1. The evil men were saved because they were taught the way of Christ. 2. The Lord went into heaven, but the apostles were left in the world. 3. The voice was heard, and the gospel was preached. 4. The churches were seen by the faithful men, and they went into them with their children. 5. You became a disciple of the Lord because his love was known by you. 6. Stones were taken from the desert and thrown into the houses of the men of God. 7. The books were written, and the messengers were sent to sinners. 8. Now the words of Christ are being heard, but then he himself shall be heard and seen in heaven. 9. After these things he was received up into glory. 10. The Son of God was glorified, and the sinners were saved. 11. You were sinners, but you became sons. 12. His word shall be preached in the world, and children shall be cleansed from their sins.

LESSON 19

THIRD DECLENSION:
LIQUID, MUTE, AND SYNCOPATED STEMS

60. Lexical Study

αἰών, αἰῶνος, ὁ, age[1]
ἄρχων, ἄρχοντος, ὁ, ruler
ἐλπίς, ἐλπίδος, ἡ, hope
νύξ, νυκτός, ἡ, night
σάρξ, σαρκός, ἡ, flesh
χάρις, χάριτος, ἡ, grace

πατήρ, πατρός, ὁ, father
μήτηρ, μητρός, ἡ, mother
θυγάτηρ, θυγατρός, ἡ, daughter
ἀρχή, ἡ, beginning
ἀγγελία, ἡ, message
κοινωνία, ἡ, fellowship

61. Grammatical Study

(1) The third declension offers a variety of inflection. For the most part the endings are regular, but the *stem* varies from one class of nouns to another. The stem is to be found in the genitive singular, which is always given with the nominative in the vocabulary. Strike off the -ος ending from the genitive singular, and the stem is left. To this stem add the endings indicated. These are the regular endings:

Singular

	Masc. and Fem.	*Neuter*
N.	ς (or none)	none
G. & A.	ος	ος
D., L., & I.	ι (short)	ι (short)
A.	ν or α (short)	none
V.	none	none

---

[1]εἰς τὸν αἰῶνα is an idiom meaning "forever." εἰς τοὺς αἰῶνας τῶν αἰώνων is an idiom meaning "forever and ever."

Plural

N. & V.	ες		a (short)
G. & A.	ων		ων
D., L., & I.	σι (short)		σι (short)
A.	ας (short)		a (short)

(2) Paradigms of third declension nouns:

Liquid		Mute		Syncopated

Singular

N. αἰών	ἐλπίς	χάρις	νύξ	πατήρ
G. αἰῶνος	ἐλπίδος	χάριτος	νυκτός	πατρός
A. αἰῶνος	ἐλπίδος	χάριτος	νυκτός	πατρός
D. αἰῶνι	ἐλπίδι	χάριτι	νυκτί	πατρί
L. αἰῶνι	ἐλπίδι	χάριτι	νυκτί	πατρί
I. αἰῶνι	ἐλπίδι	χάριτι	νυκτί	πατρί
A. αἰῶνα	ἐλπίδα	χάριν	νύκτα	πατέρα
V. αἰών	ἐλπίς	χάρις	νύξ	πάτερ

Plural

N. & V. αἰῶνες	ἐλπίδες	χάριτες	νύκτες	πατέρες
G. αἰώνων	ἐλπίδων	χαρίτων	νυκτῶν	πατέρων
A. αἰώνων	ἐλπίδων	χαρίτων	νυκτῶν	πατέρων
D. αἰῶσι	ἐλπίσι	χάρισι	νυξί	πατράσι
L. αἰῶσι	ἐλπίσι	χάρισι	νυξί	πατράσι
I. αἰῶσι	ἐλπίσι	χάρισι	νυξί	πατράσι
A. αἰῶνας	ἐλπίδας	χάριτας	νύκτας	πατέρας

(3) Analysis of third declension inflection:

There are five major classes of third declension nouns: liquid, mute, syncopated, vowel stem, and neuter. Within these are other divisions, particularly in the vowel stems and neuter nouns, both of which will be considered in the next lesson. There is a basic change in the third inflected form plural (dative, locative, and instrumental) in third declension nouns with a stem ending in a consonant. This is due to the σι ending. The harsh sound caused the Greeks to make certain changes as follows:

77

π, β or φ + σι becomes ψι.

κ, γ or χ + σι becomes ξι.

τ, δ or θ drops out leaving σι.

ν drops out leaving σι.

ντ drops out leaving σι and because *two* consonants are lost the vowel preceding ντ is lengthened; ο lengthens to ου rather than ω. Example: ἄρχοντσι becomes ἄρχουσι. All these third plural inflected forms may take movable ν.

The liquid stem nouns (nouns with the stem ending in a liquid consonant) are mostly masculine with a few feminines. Both will be declined like αἰών in the paradigm above; find the stem in the genitive singular and add the endings as indicated. ρ before σι in the third plural form does not drop out.

The mute stem nouns, some are masculine and some feminine, are represented in the above paradigms by χάρις, ἐλπίς, and νύξ. Three nouns are used for reasons which will be obvious in the discussion which follows. Note that ἐλπίς and χάρις are declined exactly alike except in the accusative singular. In this form one uses the ending α added to the full stem while the other uses the ending ν added to the shortened stem. This raises the question, "When is α used in the accusative singular and when ν?" The answer is found in the following rule: When a noun stem ends in τ, δ, or θ preceded by ι or υ and *not* accented on the ultima in the nominative form, the accusative singular has the ν ending, and the mute consonant drops out. Study ἐλπίς and χάρις in the light of this rule. The noun νύξ is included as an example of monosyllabic nouns of the third declension. These are not all mutes; some are liquid stems. In all cases the following accent principle is to be observed: Monosyllabic nouns of the third declension accent the ultima in all forms except nominative plural and accusative singular and plural.

The syncopated nouns, some are masculine and some feminine, are so called because of the shifting of the regular accent. A close study of πατήρ above will indicate just how much this accent is shifted. The term is borrowed from the field of music in which syncopation is defined as "the shifting of the regular metric accent," i.e., the tone starts on an unaccented beat and continues through to the following accented beat. The following analysis of the syncopated noun will indicate its highly inflected nature:

1. The stem is found by changing the η to ε in the nominative singular. This is unusual for a third declension noun.
2. The second (gen. and abl.) and third (dat., loc., ins.) forms singular drop the ε of the stem and accent the ultima.
3. The vocative singular is the simple stem of the noun and the accent is recessive.
4. The stem vowel is accented in all plural forms.
5. The third (dat., loc., ins.) form plural drops the stem vowel ε and inserts a short α before the σι ending.
6. This analysis is true of all syncopated nouns except ἀνήρ (man) which is so irregular that it is omitted from this study. Its forms in the Greek New Testament are best learned by observation.

62. Practical Application

(1) Translate the following sentences:

1. ἐλπίδα οὐκ ἔχομεν ὅτι οὐ γινώσκομεν τὸν Κύριον. 2. τῇ χάριτι αὐτοῦ ὁ Θεὸς ἔσωσεν ἁμαρτωλούς. 3. ὁ λόγος μου μένει εἰς τὸν αἰῶνα. 4. ὁ ἀπόστολος οὐκέτι γινώσκει τὸν Κύριον κατὰ τὴν σάρκα. 5. ὁ πονηρὸς μαθητὴς ἐξῆλθε καὶ ἦν νύξ. 6. ἄρχων ἦλθε πρὸς τὸν Χριστὸν καὶ ἐδιδάχθη τὴν ὁδὸν τῆς ζωῆς. 7. λέγομεν ὅτι ἔχομεν κοινωνίαν μετ᾽ αὐτοῦ. 8. αὕτη ἐστὶν ἡ ἀγγελία τῆς ἀληθείας · ὁ Θεός ἐστιν ἀγαθὸς καὶ οἱ υἱοὶ μένουσιν ἐν αὐτῷ εἰς τοὺς αἰῶνας τῶν αἰώνων. 9. ἐν ἀρχῇ ἦν ὁ Λόγος, καὶ ὁ Λόγος ἦν πρὸς τὸν Θεόν, καὶ Θεὸς ἦν ὁ Λόγος. Οὗτος ἦν ἐν ἀρχῇ πρὸς τὸν Θεόν. πάντα δι᾽ αὐτοῦ ἐγένετο. 10. ὁ Κύριος διδάσκει ὅτι ὁ Θεός ἐστιν ὁ πατὴρ ἀγαθῶν ἀνθρώπων. 11. ὁ υἱὸς καὶ ἡ θυγάτηρ λαμβάνουσι καλὰ δῶρα ἀπὸ τῆς μητρὸς αὐτῶν. 12. ἀγάπη καὶ ἐλπὶς μένουσι εἰς τὸν αἰῶνα.

(2) Translate the following sentences:

1. The Son of God is the ruler of his kingdom. 2. The faithful disciples preached the gospel in the night and in the day. 3. The flesh is evil, but it will be cleansed from sin by the grace of God. 4. From the beginning of our fellowship with him we knew peace. 5. The daughter was taught the love of God by her mother,

and the son by his father. 6. We were wicked men, but we were saved by his grace and love. 7. Through the death of the Son we see the love of the Father. 8. The world shall be destroyed, but the kingdom of heaven abides forever and ever. 9. The message of his church brings love, truth, grace, and hope. 10. The Son was raised from death by the Father, and now men have hope of life after death.

LESSON 20

THIRD DECLENSION: VOWEL STEM NOUNS

63. Lexical Study

ἀνάστασις, ἀναστάσεως, ἡ, resurrection
γνῶσις, γνώσεως, ἡ, knowledge
δύναμις, δυνάμεως, ἡ, power
κρίσις, κρίσεως, ἡ, judgment
πίστις, πίστεως, ἡ, faith
πόλις, πόλεως, ἡ, city
στάσις, στάσεως, ἡ, dissension
ἁλιεύς, ἁλιέως, ὁ, fisherman
ἀρχιερεύς, ἀρχιερέως, ὁ, chief priest
βασιλεύς, βασιλέως, ὁ, king
γραμματεύς, γραμματέως, ὁ, scribe
ἱερεύς, ἱερέως, ὁ, priest
ἰχθύς, ἰχθύος, ὁ, fish
στάχυς, στάχυος, ὁ, ear of corn

64. Grammatical Study

(1) The ι stem nouns of the third declension are *all* feminine. The following paradigms are representative of this class.

Singular

N.	πίστις	δύναμις
G. & A.	πίστεως	δυνάμεως
D., L., & I.	πίστει	δυνάμει
A.	πίστιν	δύναμιν
V.	πίστι	δύναμι

81

Plural

N. & V.	πίστεις	δυνάμεις
G. & A.	πίστεων	δυνάμεων
D., L., & I.	πίστεσι	δυνάμεσι
A.	πίστεις	δυνάμεις

The following analysis calls attention to the characteristics of the inflection of these nouns:

1. Find the stem by striking off the ς in the nominative singular.

2. ε replaces the final ι except in nominative, accusative, and vocative singular.

3. ε unites with ι ending in dative (etc.) singular to form a diphthong.

4. εις in nominative plural and accusative plural is the result of the contraction of εες and εας respectively.

5. The accent of the second inflected form (gen. and abl.) singular and plural is irregular and stands on the *antepenult* even with a long ultima.

(2) The ευ stem nouns of third declension are *all* masculine. Note closely the inflection in the following paradigm:

Singular		Plural	
N.	ἱερεύς	N. & V.	ἱερεῖς
G. & A.	ἱερέως	G. & A.	ἱερέων
D., L., & I.	ἱερεῖ	D., L., & I.	ἱερεῦσι
A.	ἱερέα	A.	ἱερεῖς
V.	ἱερεῦ		

These features should be noted in the analysis of the inflection of this class.

1. Find the stem by striking off the ς of the nominative singular.

2. The final υ of the stem is dropped before an ending with a vowel.

3. In the dative (etc.) singular and the nominative and accusative plural the same combinations as are found in the ι stem nouns appear.

82

(3) The υ stem nouns of the third declension are mostly masculine; there are a few feminines and one neuter (δάκρυ, a tear). Note the inflection which is entirely regular. The stem is found by dropping the ς of the nominative singular.

	Singular		Plural	
N.	ἰχθύς	N. & V.	ἰχθύες
G. & A.	ἰχθύος	G. & A.	ἰχθύων
D., L., & I.	ἰχθύι	D., L., & I.	ἰχθύσι
A.	ἰχθύν	A.	ἰχθύας
V.	ἰχθύ		(sometimes ἰχθῦς)

65. Practical Application

(1) Translate the following sentences:

1. οἱ μαθηταὶ τοῦ Κυρίου ἐσθίουσι ἄρτον καὶ ἰχθὺν καὶ στάχυας. 2. ὁ Μεσσίας ἐκήρυσσε τὸ εὐαγγέλιον τοῖς ἁλιεῦσι καὶ οἱ ἀρχιερεῖς καὶ οἱ γραμματεῖς ἔπεμπον τοὺς δούλους αὐτῶν ἀκούειν αὐτόν. 3. ἐσώθημεν τῇ χάριτι διὰ πίστεως. 4. ἐν τῇ πόλει ὁ βασιλεὺς μένει, οἱ δὲ ἁλιεῖς παρὰ τῇ θαλάσσῃ. 5. ὁ Θεὸς ἔχει τὴν δύναμιν κρίσεως ἐν τῷ κόσμῳ καὶ ἐν τῷ οὐρανῷ. 6. οἱ ἱερεῖς γινώσκουσι τὸν νόμον, ἀλλ᾽ οὐ γινώσκουσι χάριν καὶ πίστιν. 7. ἐν τῇ ἀναστάσει τοῦ Χριστοῦ ἐλάβομεν ζωὴν καὶ εἰρήνην. 8. στάσις ἐν τῇ ἐκκλησίᾳ ἐστὶ κακή. 9. ὁ βασιλεὺς ὁ ἀγαθὸς βλέπει τὴν ἡμέραν τοῦ Κυρίου. 10. λήμψεσθε δύναμιν ἀπὸ τοῦ Θεοῦ καὶ ἔσεσθε οἱ μαθηταὶ αὐτοῦ.

(2) Translate the following sentences:

1. The chief priests and the scribes went out of the temple to hear the Lord. 2. The Lord spoke a parable to the fishermen, and they became his disciples. 3. The disciples were eating corn, and the priests saw them. 4. Even the children of the wicked men have the knowledge of God's grace in their hearts. 5. You were cleansed from your sins by grace through faith. 6. I have heard the parable concerning the judgment, and I received its truth into my heart. 7. By the resurrection of Christ from death the power of the Father is being glorified. 8. The king judges his servants, but we are under the power of the Lord. 9. By the law comes the knowledge of the power of sin. 10. Dissension was in the city on account of the parable concerning light and darkness.

83

LESSON 21

THIRD DECLENSION: NEUTER NOUNS

66. Lexical Study

βάθος, βάθους, τό, depth
γένος, γένους, τό, race
ἔθνος, ἔθνους, τό, nation[1]
ἔθος, ἔθους, τό, custom
ἔλεος, ἐλέους, τό, mercy
ὄρος, ὄρους, τό, mountain
σκότος, σκότους, τό, darkness
τέλος, τέλους, τό, end

αἷμα, αἵματος, τό, blood
θέλημα, θελήματος, τό, will
ὄνομα, ὀνόματος, τό, name
πνεῦμα, πνεύματος, τό, spirit
ῥῆμα, ῥήματος, τό, word
στόμα, στόματος, τό, mouth
σῶμα, σώματος, τό, body
ὕδωρ, ὕδατος, τό, water

67. Grammatical Study

(1) The nouns in the first column of the above vocabulary are known as ες stem nouns because the stem really ends in that combination. In the actual inflection of the noun so many contractions have taken place that the basic stem is hardly seen. Review the neuter endings for third declension nouns in paragraph 61 (1). Note the use of these endings and the changes in form in the following paradigm. The stem is γενεσ-

Singular

	Original form	Form actually used
N. & V.	γένες	γένος
G. & A.	γένεσος	γένους
D. L., & I.	γένεσι	γένει
A.	γένες	γένος

---

[1] In the plural this is often translated "Gentiles."

84

Plural

N. & V.	γένεσα	γένη
G. & A.	γενέσων	γενῶν
D. L., & I.	γένεσσι	γένεσι
A.	γένεσα	γένη

These changes are due to the loss of the σ in many of the forms and a resulting contraction of the ε with the case ending. For practical usage the student should learn the "forms actually used" since the "original forms" do not appear in the New Testament. All third declension neuter nouns with the genitive singular ending in ους will be declined like γένος.

(2) The nouns in the second column of the above vocabulary are known as ατ stem nouns. Strike off the ος of the genitive singular and the stem remains. The endings are added regularly. Note the short forms in the nominative and accusative singular, and the loss of the stem τ before σι in the dative plural. All ατ stem neuter nouns will be declined like σῶμα.

	Singular	Plural
N. & V.	σῶμα	σώματα
G. & A.	σώματος	σωμάτων
D. L., & I.	σώματι	σώμασι
A.	σῶμα	σώματα

68. Practical Application

Translate the following sentences:

1. γινώσκομεν καὶ τὸ θέλημα καὶ τὴν ἀγάπην τοῦ Θεοῦ. 2. ὁ Κύριος εἰσῆλθεν εἰς τὸ ἱερὸν κατὰ τὸ ἔθος αὐτοῦ. 3. ὁ Χριστὸς ἐδίδασκε τοὺς ὄχλους ἐν τῷ ὄρει. 4. τὸ σῶμα τοῦ Κυρίου ἐδοξάσθη μετὰ τὴν ἀνάστασιν. 5. ἐν τῷ ὀνόματι τοῦ Χριστοῦ ἔχομεν ἐλπίδα τῆς ζωῆς. 6. ἐσώθημεν διὰ τοῦ αἵματος τοῦ υἱοῦ τοῦ Θεοῦ καὶ νῦν γινώσκομεν τὸ ἔλεος αὐτοῦ. 7. ἤκουσαν τὰ ῥήματα τοῦ στόματος αὐτοῦ καὶ ἔλαβον τὸ ἔλεος αὐτοῦ. 8. τὰ ἔθνη οὐ γινώσκει τὸ βάθος τοῦ ἐλέους τοῦ Θεοῦ. 9. ἡμεῖς ἐβαπτίσθημεν ὑπὸ τοῦ Χριστοῦ, ὑμεῖς δὲ ἐβαπτίσθητε ὑπ᾽ ἀποστόλου αὐτοῦ. 10. οἱ μαθηταὶ ἐβάπτιζον ἐν τῷ ὀνόματι τοῦ πατρὸς καὶ τοῦ υἱοῦ καὶ τοῦ πνεύματος. 11. οἱ

πονηροὶ μένουσιν ἐν τῷ σκότει τῆς ἁμαρτίας, οἱ δὲ πιστοὶ ἀκούουσι τὰ ῥήματα τοῦ Κυρίου καὶ γίνονται ἀγαθοὶ μαθηταί. 12. ἐγὼ μὲν βαπτίζω ὑμᾶς ἐν ὕδατι, ἐκεῖνος δὲ βαπτίσει ὑμᾶς ἐν τῷ πνεύματι.

English into Greek exercises will be omitted in the remainder of this text. The teacher may use his own exercises or augment the above Greek into English exercises as he sees the need.

LESSON 22

PRESENT PARTICIPLES

69. Lexical Study

ὀφείλω, I owe, I ought

ψεύδομαι, I lie, I deceive

φαίνω, I shine, I cause to shine

ἀδικία, ἡ, unrighteousness

ἱλασμός, ὁ, propitiation

Ἰησοῦς, ὁ, Jesus[1]

ὀφθαλμός, ὁ, eye

παράκλητος, ὁ, advocate

σκάνδαλον, τό, stumbling block

χείρ, χειρός, ἡ, hand

ψεύστης, ὁ, liar

φῶς, φωτός, τό, light

70. Grammatical Study

(1) The present active participle of λύω is:

Singular

	M.	F.	N.
N. & V.	λύων	λύουσα	λῦον
G. & A.	λύοντος	λυούσης	λύοντος
D., L., & I.	λύοντι	λυούσῃ	λύοντι
A.	λύοντα	λύουσαν	λῦον

Plural

	M.	F.	N.
N. & V.	λύοντες	λύουσαι	λύοντα
G. & A.	λυόντων	λυουσῶν	λυόντων
D., L., & I.	λύουσι(ν)	λυούσαις	λύουσι(ν)
A.	λύοντας	λυούσας	λύοντα

[1]This is an irregular noun of the second declension; it has only three forms in the New Testament: nom., Ἰησοῦς; gen., abl., dat., loc., ins., and voc., Ἰησοῦ; acc., Ἰησοῦν.

(2) The present middle and passive participle of λύω is:

Singular

	M.	F.	N.
N. & V.	λυόμενος	λυομένη	λυόμενον
G. & A.	λυομένου	λυομένης	λυομένου
D., L., & I.	λυομένῳ	λυομένῃ	λυομένῳ
A.	λυόμενον	λυομένην	λυόμενον

Plural

	M.	F.	N.
N. & V.	λυόμενοι	λυόμεναι	λυόμενα
G. & A.	λυομένων	λυομένων	λυομένων
D., L., & I.	λυομένοις	λυομέναις	λυομένοις
A.	λυομένους	λυομένας	λυόμενα

(3) The present participle of εἰμί is:

Singular

	M.	F.	N.
N. & V.	ὤν	οὖσα	ὄν
G. & A.	ὄντος	οὔσης	ὄντος
D., L., & I.	ὄντι	οὔσῃ	ὄντι
A.	ὄντα	οὖσαν	ὄν

Plural

	M.	F.	N.
N. & V.	ὄντες	οὖσαι	ὄντα
G. & A.	ὄντων	οὐσῶν	ὄντων
D., L., & I.	οὖσι(ν)	οὔσαις	οὖσι(ν)
A.	ὄντας	οὔσας	ὄντα

(4) The participle is a verbal adjective. The present active participle is declined like a third declension mute stem noun in the masculine and neuter and like a first declension σ stem noun in the feminine. Study carefully the inflection and accenting of the present active participle of λύω. The present active participle of any regular verb may be formed by adding the above endings to the stem.

The present middle and passive participle forms are identical but the function is different. The characteristic of this construction is the middle and passive suffix μεν, which is added to the stem by means of the connecting vowel *o*. The masculine and neuter are declined like masculine and neuter nouns of the second declension, and the feminine is declined like any η ending noun of the first declension. Observe carefully the accenting and inflection of the above paradigm. Add the -όμενος, η, ον endings to any regular verb and the present middle and passive forms are made. Deponent verbs will, of course, take this system for the present participle.

The present participle of εἰμί is the inflected system of endings found in the present active participle. Note the accent in these forms.

(5) The characteristics of participles:

    1. As a *verb* the participle:
      a. has tense and voice
      b. may take an object
      c. may be an adverbial modifier

    2. As an *adjective* the participle:
      a. has case, gender, and number
      b. may be used substantively
      c. may be used as an adjective modifier

(6) The function of participles:

The *verbal* function of participles is to be noted in relation to the above characteristics. *Voice* is the same here as in other verbal forms, i.e., is the subject acting (active), being acted upon (passive), or acting so as to participate in the results of the action (middle). In *tense* the participle has to do with *kind* of action. The present participle indicates continuous action, the aorist participle indicates punctiliar action, etc. Only four of the Greek tenses have participles: present, aorist, future, and perfect. The *time* of action in participles is indicated in the relation of the action of the participle to the action of the main verb. The following indicates that relationship: The aorist participle indicates action which is antecedent to the action of the main verb.

The present participle indicates action which is contemporaneous with the action of the main verb. The future participle indicates action which is subsequent to the action of the main verb. The perfect participle indicates action which has come to be a state of being. These distinctions will become clearer as the other participles are studied. For the time being it is sufficient to know that the present participle indicates *continuous* action which takes place at the *same time* as the action of the main verb. Examples: (1) λέγων ταῦτα ὁ ἄνθρωπος βλέπει τὸν Κύριον. "While saying these things, the man sees the Lord." (2) διδασκόμενος ὑπὸ τοῦ Κυρίου ὁ ἄνθρωπος λαμβάνει τὴν ἀλήθειαν. "While being taught by the Lord, the man receives the truth" or "as the man is being taught by the Lord, he receives the truth."

The first of these examples illustrates another characteristic of the participle. ταῦτα is accusative as the direct object of the participle λέγων.

The use of the participle as an adverbial modifier may be seen in this illustration: ἐρχόμενοι ἐκήρυσσον τὸ εὐαγγέλιον. "As they were going, they were preaching the gospel." The participle modifies the verb and tells *when* they were preaching — "as they were going." As an adverbial modifier the participle may tell when, how, why, on what condition, by what means, or under what circumstances an action took place. This will be studied in greater detail in connection with subordinate clauses.

The *adjectival* function of participles is likewise indicated by the above characteristics. As an adjective the participle agrees with the noun it modifies in gender, number, and case. Check this agreement in the examples used in the preceding paragraphs.

As an adjective the participle may be used substantivally; i.e., as a noun. Just as ὁ ἀγαθός means "the good man," ὁ λύων means "the loosing man"; translated into smooth English it means "the man who looses" or "he who looses." The relative translation must be followed to give the full significance of the construction.

Study these examples:

(1) βλέπω τὸν λέγοντα ταῦτα. "I see the one who is saying these things." (2) ἔβλεψα τὸν λέγοντα ταῦτα. "I saw the one who was saying these things." (3) βλέπω τοὺς λέγοντας ταῦτα. "I see the

men who (or those who) are saying these things." (4) βλέπω τὸν ἀδελφὸν τῆς λεγούσης ταῦτα. "I see the brother of the woman who is saying these things."

As an adjective the participle may be used as an adjectival modifier. In this construction the participle is always in the attributive position with the noun and is *usually* the longer of the two possible forms. Thus either ὁ λέγων ἀπόστολος or ὁ ἀπόστολος ὁ λέγων means "the saying apostle," but the second is the usual form: ὁ ἀπόστολος ὁ λέγων ταῦτα, "the apostle who is saying these things."

This introduces a very important matter in the function of participles. When the participle is in the *attributive* position (has the article), it is to be given a *relative* translation: "the one who," "he who," or "she who." When the participle is in the predicate position (does not have the article), it is to be given a *temporal* translation — "while" or "as." Check this difference in the following examples: (1) ἔβλεψα τὸν ἀπόστολον λέγοντα ταῦτα. "I saw the apostle while he was saying these things." (2) ἔβλεψα τὸν ἀπόστολον τὸν λέγοντα ταῦτα. "I saw the apostle who was saying these things." The first example tells *when* the apostle was seen; the second tells *which* apostle was seen.

71. Practical Application

Translate the following sentences:

1. ὁ δεχόμενος σὲ δέχεται καὶ τὸν Κύριον. 2. ταῦτα εἶπον τοῖς εἰσερχομένοις εἰς τὴν ἐκκλησίαν. 3. εἰσερχόμενος εἰς τὴν ἐκκλησίαν ἔλεγε τὴν παραβολὴν ὑμῖν. 4. αἱ ἐκκλησίαι αἱ λυόμεναι ὑπὸ τοῦ πονηροῦ ἄρχοντος δοξάζονται ὑπὸ τοῦ Κυρίου. 5. οἱ λαμβάνοντες τὴν χάριν τοῦ Θεοῦ σώζονται. 6. ἀναγινώσκομεν τὰ γραφόμενα ἐν τῷ βιβλίῳ τῆς ζωῆς. 7. τοῦτό ἐστι τὸ πνεῦμα τὸ σῶζον ὑμᾶς καὶ καθαρίζον ὑμᾶς ἀπὸ τῶν ἁμαρτιῶν ὑμῶν. 8. τὸ φῶς τοῦ Θεοῦ φαίνει ἐν τῷ κόσμῳ. 9. ὁ λέγων ὅτι ἔχει κοινωνίαν μετὰ τοῦ Θεοῦ ἀλλὰ μένει ἐν τῷ σκότει ἁμαρτίας ἐστὶ ψεύστης. 10. Ἰησοῦς Χριστός ἐστιν ὁ δίκαιος παράκλητος ἡμῶν. 11. ὁ Θεὸς φῶς ἐστιν καὶ σκοτία ἐν αὐτῷ οὐκ ἔστιν. 12. ἦσαν ἐν τῷ οἴκῳ τῷ λυομένῳ. 13. ἐν τοῖς ὀφθαλμοῖς αὐτοῦ ὁ ἀπόστολος εἶδε τὰς χεῖρας τοῦ Κυρίου μετὰ τὴν ἀνάστασιν. 14. οἱ ὄντες υἱοὶ τοῦ Θεοῦ ὀφείλουσι μένειν ἐν τῷ λόγῳ αὐτοῦ. 15. εἴδομεν τὸν ἀπόστολον ὄντα ἐν τῇ ἐκκλησίᾳ·

LESSON 23

AORIST ACTIVE AND MIDDLE PARTICIPLES

72. Lexical Study

διώκω, I persecute
μή, *adv.*, not (*with moods other than the indicative*)
μηδέ, *conj.*, and not, nor, not even (*used like* μή)
μηδέ — μηδέ, *conj.*, neither — nor (*used like* μή)
μηκέτι, *adv.*, no longer (*used like* μή)

Study paragraph 73 carefully, and then go back over all verbs used up to this point and form the aorist participles. Note: εἰπών is second aorist active participle for εἶπον, and ἰδών is second aorist active participle for εἶδον.

73. Grammatical Study

(1) The first aorist active participle of λύω is:

Singular

	M.	F.	N.
N. & V.	λύσας	λύσασα	λῦσαν
G. & A.	λύσαντος	λυσάσης	λύσαντος
D., L., & I.	λύσαντι	λυσάσῃ	λύσαντι
A.	λύσαντα	λύσασαν	λῦσαν

Plural

	M.	F.	N.
N. & V.	λύσαντες	λύσασαι	λύσαντα
G. & A.	λυσάντων	λυσασῶν	λυσάντων
D., L., & I.	λύσασι(ν)	λυσάσαις	λύσασι(ν)
A.	λύσαντας	λυσάσας	λύσαντα

(2) The first aorist middle participle of λύω is:

Singular

	M.	F.	N.
N. & V.	λυσάμενος	λυσαμένη	λυσάμενον
G. & A.	λυσαμένου	λυσαμένης	λυσαμένου
D., L., & I.	λυσαμένῳ	λυσαμένῃ	λυσαμένῳ
A.	λυσάμενον	λυσαμένην	λυσάμενον

Plural

	M.	F.	N.
N. & V.	λυσάμενοι	λυσάμεναι	λυσάμενα
G. & A.	λυσαμένων	λυσαμένων	λυσαμένων
D., L., & I.	λυσαμένοις	λυσαμέναις	λυσαμένοις
A	λυσαμένους	λυσαμένας	λυσάμενα

(3) The second aorist active participle of λείπω is:

Singular

	M.	F.	N.
N. & V.	λιπών	λιποῦσα	λιπόν
G. & A.	λιπόντος	λιπούσης	λιπόντος
D., L., & I.	λιπόντι	λιπούσῃ	λιπόντι
A.	λιπόντα	λιποῦσαν	λιπόν

Plural

	M.	F.	N.
N. & V	λιπόντες	λιποῦσαι	λιπόντα
G. & A.	λιπόντων	λιπουσῶν	λιπόντων
D., L., & I.	λιποῦσι(ν)	λιπούσαις	λιποῦσι(ν)
A.	λιπόντας	λιπούσας	λιπόντα

(4) The second aorist middle participle of λείπω is:

Singular

	M.	F.	N.
N. & V.	λιπόμενος	λιπομένη	λιπόμενον
G. & A.	λιπομένου	λιπομένης	λιπομένου
D., L., & I.	λιπομένῳ	λιπομένῃ	λιπομένῳ
A.	λιπόμενον	λιπομένην	λιπόμενον

93

Plural

N. & V.	λιπόμενοι	λιπόμεναι	λιπόμενα
G. & A.	λιπομένων	λιπομένων	λιπομένων
D., L., & I.	λιπομένοις	λιπομέναις	λιπομένοις
A.	λιπομένους	λιπομένας	λιπόμενα

(5) Like the aorist indicative the aorist participle is formed on the aorist stem. There is no augment for reasons which will be indicated later.

The first aorist active participle has the first aorist σα- tense suffix added to the stem. Example λυσα-. Following this the participle is declined in masculine and neuter like a mute stem noun of the third declension and in the feminine like a σ stem noun of the first declension. Observe this in paradigm (1) above. The first aorist middle (the passive is entirely different) consists of the aorist stem λυσα- plus the middle participle suffix -μεν- plus the second declension endings in masculine and neuter and first declension endings in the feminine. In other words, the first aorist middle participle is like the present middle participle except for the tense suffix σα added to the stem. Observe this in paradigm (2) above.

The second aorist participle is built on the second aorist stem. It is declined exactly like the present participle except that in the second aorist active participle the accent is irregular. It appears on the ultima in the nominative masculine singular (λιπών) and thereafter follows the noun rule. Observe the accent and inflection in paradigms (3) and (4) above in comparison with the same forms in the present participle.

(6) The *kind* of action in the aorist participle is punctiliar, i.e., finished action. The *time* of action is antecedent to the action of the main verb; therefore, the time of action is a relative matter. The main thing stressed in verbs other than the indicative mood is the *kind* of action. For this reason the augment, which indicates action in past time, is absent in participles, infinitives, subjunctives, etc.

Voice in the aorist participle is the same as in other forms, i.e., it indicates the relation of the subject to the action.

The use of the participle with or without the article is the same here as in the present participle. In translation the aorist participle should be put into good English idiom. Examples: λύσας is to be translated "having loosed," "when he had loosed," or "after he had loosed." ὁ λύσας is to be translated "the one who loosed," "he who loosed," etc. Observe carefully the following illustrations, noting the temporal or relative use and the relation of the action of the participle to that of the main verb.

1. ὁ ἄνθρωπος εἰπὼν ταῦτα βλέπει τὸν Κύριον. "The man, having said these things, is seeing the Lord."

2. εἰπὼν ταῦτα ἐξῆλθεν ἐκ τοῦ οἴκου. "Having said these things, he went out of the house," or "after he had said," or "when he had said," etc.

3. ὁ ἄνθρωπος ὁ εἰπὼν ταῦτα ἦλθεν εἰς τὸν οἶκον. "The man who had said these things went into the house."

4. ὁ εἰπὼν ταῦτα ἦλθεν εἰς τὸν οἶκον. "The man who (or he who) had said these things went into the house."

74. Practical Application

Translate the following sentences:

1. ἐξελθὼν ἐκ τοῦ οἴκου ταῦτα εἶπεν. 2. πισταί εἰσιν αἱ δεξάμεναι τοὺς ἀποστόλους τοὺς διωκομένους. 3. ὁ μὴ ἰδὼν τὸν Κύριον οὐκ ἐπίστευσεν εἰς αὐτόν. 4. ἔτι ὢν ἐν τῇ ὁδῷ ὁ Κύριος εἶπε ταῦτα τοῖς ἐξελθοῦσιν ἐκ τοῦ οἴκου καὶ πορευομένοις μετ᾽ αὐτοῦ πρὸς τὴν ἐκκλησίαν. 5. πονηροὶ ἦσαν οἱ ἄγγελοι οἱ πεσόντες ἐκ τοῦ οὐρανοῦ. 6. κηρύσσομεν περὶ τοῦ σώσαντος ἡμᾶς καὶ καθαρίσαντος ἡμᾶς ἀπὸ τῶν ἁμαρτιῶν ἡμῶν. 7. συναγαγόντες οἱ μαθηταὶ ἐδόξασαν τὸ ὄνομα τοῦ Θεοῦ. 8. τὰ τέκνα τὰ λαβόντα ταῦτα ἀπὸ τῶν ἀκουσάντων τοῦ Χριστοῦ εἶδεν αὐτὸν ἔτι ὄντα ἐν τῷ κόσμῳ. 9. οὗτοί εἰσιν οἱ κηρύξαντες τὸ εὐαγγέλιον τῆς ἀγάπης, ἀλλ᾽ ἐκεῖνοί εἰσιν οἱ διώξαντες τοὺς πιστεύοντας αὐτό. 10. δεξάμενοι ἄρτον ἀπὸ τοῦ Μεσσίου οἱ ὄχλοι ἀπῆλθον εἰς τὴν πόλιν. 11. ἀκούσαντες τῶν λεγομένων ὑπὸ τοῦ ἀποστόλου τοῦ Χριστοῦ τοῦ υἱοῦ τοῦ Θεοῦ, ἐπίστευσαν εἰς αὐτὸν καὶ ἔλαβον τὴν χάριν αὐτοῦ.

LESSON 24

AORIST PASSIVE PARTICIPLES

75. Lexical Study

ἅγιος, α, ον, holy[1]   ἐπιθυμία, ἡ, lust
λοιπός, ή, όν, remaining[2]   συναγωγή, ἡ, synagogue
μακάριος, α, ον, blessed   σωτηρία, ἡ, salvation

Study paragraph 76 closely, and then form the aorist passive participle nominative masculine singular of all verbs studied up to here.

76. Grammatical Study

(1) The aorist passive participle of λύω is:

Singular

	M.	F.	N.
N. & V.	λυθείς	λυθεῖσα	λυθέν
G. & A.	λυθέντος	λυθείσης	λυθέντος
D., L., & I.	λυθέντι	λυθείσῃ	λυθέντι
A.	λυθέντα	λυθεῖσαν	λυθέν

Plural

	M.	F.	N.
N. & V.	λυθέντες	λυθεῖσαι	λυθέντα
G. & A.	λυθέντων	λυθεισῶν	λυθέντων
D., L., & I.	λυθεῖσι	λυθείσαις	λυθεῖσι
A.	λυθέντας	λυθείσας	λυθέντα

---

[1] οἱ ἅγιοι used substantively means "the saints."
[2] οἱ λοιποί used substantively means "the rest," i.e., "the remaining persons."

96

(2) Any aorist passive participle will be declined like λύω. Drop the augment from the aorist passive stem and add the endings -εις, -εισα, -εν, etc. Note that the first aorist passive participle will have θ as a tense suffix; second aorist passive participles will not have θ. The accent starts on the ultima in the nominative masculine singular and then follows the noun rule. The masculine and neuter are declined like third declension mute stem nouns; the feminine is declined like first declension σ stem nouns.

(3) The aorist passive participle is used like the other participles. The *kind* of action is punctiliar; the *time* of action is antecedent to that of the main verb. The voice indicates that the subject receives the action.

The participle may be translated several ways. ὁ λυθεὶς ἄνθρωπος ἐξῆλθεν ἐκ τοῦ οἴκου could be translated: "The man who was loosed went out of the house" or "The man who had been loosed went out of the house." σωθεὶς δοξάσει τὸν Κύριον is best translated: "Having been saved, he will praise the Lord" or "After he has been saved, he will praise the Lord." The use of the word in its context must determine the translation. Compare the translations in the following summary.

The participle without the article (temporal)

Present	Act.	λύων	loosing; while loosing; as he was loosing
	Mid.	λυόμενος	loosing for himself; while, etc.; as, etc.
	Pass.	λυόμενος	being loosed; while, etc.; as, etc.
Aorist	Act.	λύσας	having loosed; after he had loosed; when he had loosed.
	Mid.	λυσάμενος	having loosed for himself; after, etc.; when, etc.
	Pass.	λυθείς	having been loosed; when he was loosed, when he has been, when he had been; after he was —, after he has been —; after he had been.

The participle with the article (relative)

	Act.	ὁ λύων	he who looses; the man who; the one who
Present	Mid.	ὁ λυόμενος	he who looses for himself; the man who; the one who, etc.
	Pass.	ὁ λυόμενος	he who is being loosed; the man who; the one who, etc.
	Act.	ὁ λύσας	he (the man, the one) who loosed, has loosed, or had loosed.
Aorist	Mid.	ὁ λυσάμενος	he (the man, the one) who loosed for himself; has, etc.; had, etc.
	Pass.	ὁ λυθείς	he (the man, the one) who was loosed; has been, etc.; had been, etc.

(4) A construction frequently found in the Greek New Testament is that known as the "genitive absolute." It is a construction which has a very loose connection with the main part of the sentence. It consists of a participle and a noun or pronoun connected with it. These are put into the genitive case when the subject of the main verb is different from the noun or pronoun used with the participle. Compare the two following sentences: (1) εἰπόντες ταῦτα οἱ ἀπόστολοι ἀπῆλθον. "Having said these things the apostles went away." The subject of the sentence, ἀπόστολοι, has a direct connection with the participle εἰπόντες, which, therefore, appears in the nominative case. (2) εἰπόντων ταῦτα τῶν μαθητῶν οἱ ἀπόστολοι ἀπῆλθον. "The disciples having said these things, the apostles went away," or "When the disciples had said these things, the apostles went away." There is no direct connection between εἰπόντων and the subject of the sentence ἀπόστολοι. In other words, the ones doing the "saying" and the ones doing the "going" are different people. The participle with its noun is, therefore, "absolute," i.e., loosed or separated from the main part of the sentence and, hence, in the genitive case. Bear in mind that the genitive absolute is used when the noun (or pronoun) going with a participle is different from the subject of the finite verb and has no direct grammatical relationship to the remainder of the sentence. Compare the following sen-

tences at this point: (1) λέγοντος αὐτοῦ ταῦτα ἀπῆλθον. "While he was saying these things, I went away." This demands the genitive absolute. (2) εἶδον αὐτὸν λέγοντα ταῦτα. "I saw him while he was saying these things." The subject of the main verb is different from the person doing the acting expressed in the participle. The genitive absolute is not used, however, because the participle has a direct grammatical relationship to the rest of the sentence. It is accusative to agree with the noun which it modifies.

77. Practical Application

Translate the following sentences:

1. εἰσελθόντων τῶν μαθητῶν εἰς τὸ πλοῖον, ὁ Κύριος ἀπῆλθεν εἰς τὸ ὄρος.
2. πιστευσάντων ὑμῶν εἰς τὸν Χριστόν, τὰ τέκνα ὑμῶν καὶ ἐπίστευσεν.
3. εἰπόντος ταῦτα τοῦ ἁγίου πνεύματος, ἐκήρυξαν τὸ εὐαγγέλιον οἱ ἀπόστολοι.
4. ἀκουσθέντος τοῦ λόγου τὸ ὄνομα τοῦ Θεοῦ ἐδοξάσθη καὶ ἐν τῇ συναγωγῇ καὶ ἐν τῇ ἐκκλησίᾳ. 5. αὕτη ἐστὶν ἡ σωτηρία ἡ κηρυχθεῖσα ἐν τῷ κόσμῳ ὑπὸ τῶν ἰδόντων Ἰησοῦν. 6. ἀναλημφθέντος τοῦ Κυρίου εἰς οὐρανὸν οἱ μαθηταὶ εἰσῆλθον εἰς τὴν πόλιν κατὰ τὴν ἐντολὴν αὐτοῦ. 7. οἱ ἀπόστολοι ἀπεστάλησαν εἰς τὰς συναγωγάς, οἱ δὲ λοιποὶ τῶν μαθητῶν μένουσιν ἐν τῇ ἐκκλησίᾳ. 8. ἐπελθόντος τοῦ ἁγίου πνεύματος ἐπ᾽ αὐτοὺς ἔλαβον δύναμιν. 9. ταῦτα εἰπὼν βλεπόντων αὐτῶν ἀνελήμφθη ἀπὸ τῶν ὀφθαλμῶν αὐτῶν εἰς οὐρανόν. 10. μακάριός ἐστιν ὁ ἰδὼν τὴν σωτηρίαν τοῦ Θεοῦ. 11. καθαρισθέντες ἀπὸ τῶν ἐπιθυμιῶν καὶ τῶν ἁμαρτιῶν ἡμῶν ἐβαπτίσθημεν εἰς τὸ ὄνομα τοῦ πατρὸς, τοῦ υἱοῦ, καὶ τοῦ πνεύματος τοῦ ἁγίου. 12. οἱ ἅγιοι συνάγουσι τοὺς ἁμαρτωλοὺς εἰς τὴν ἐκκλησίαν. 13. λέγοντος αὐτοῦ ταῦτα εἶδον τὴν ἀλήθειαν τῆς ἀγάπης τοῦ Θεοῦ. 14. τοῖς θεραπευθεῖσιν ὑπὸ τοῦ Χριστοῦ εἴπετε ῥήματα ἐλπίδος καὶ ζωῆς.

LESSON 25

PERFECT, ACTIVE, MIDDLE, AND PASSIVE INDICATIVE

78. Lexical Study

ἀκήκοα, perf. act. of ἀκούω
βεβάπτισμαι, perf. pass.
  of βαπτίζω
γέγονα, perf. act. of γίνομαι
γέγραφα, perf. act. of γράφω
ἐγγίζω, I come near
ἐγήγερμαι, perf. pass.
  of ἐγείρω

ἔγνωκα, perf. act. of γινώσκω
ἐλήλυθα, perf. act. of ἔρχομαι
λέλυκα, perf. act. of λύω
πεπίστευκα, perf. act. of
  πιστεύω
σέσωσμαι, perf. pass. of
  σώζω

79. Grammatical Study

(1) The perfect tense forms:

1. The perfect active indicative of λύω is:

λέλυκα, I have loosed
λέλυκας, you have loosed
λέλυκε(ν), he has loosed

λελύκαμεν, we have loosed
λελύκατε, you have loosed
λελύκασι, (or λέλυκαν)
  they have loosed

2. The perfect middle indicative of λύω is:

λέλυμαι, I have loosed
  for myself
λέλυσαι, you have loosed
  for yourself
λέλυται, he has loosed
  for himself

λελύμεθα, we have loosed
  for ourselves
λέλυσθε, you have loosed
  for yourselves
λέλυνται, they have loosed
  for themselves

The perfect passive indicative is the same in *form* as the middle. The translation will be "I have been loosed, you have been loosed, etc."

3. The perfect active participle of λύω is:

Singular

	M.	F.	N.
N.	λελυκώς	λελυκυῖα	λελυκός
G. & A.	λελυκότος	λελυκυίας	λελυκότος
D., L., & I.	λελυκότι	λελυκυίᾳ	λελυκότι
A.	λελυκότα	λελυκυῖαν	λελυκός

Plural

	M.	F.	N.
N.	λελυκότες	λελυκυῖαι	λελυκότα
G. & A.	λελυκότων	λελυκυιῶν	λελυκότων
D., L., & I.	λελυκόσι (ν)	λελυκυίαις	λελυκόσι (ν)
A.	λελυκότας	λελυκυίας	λελυκότα

4. The perfect middle and passive participle of λύω is:

Singular

	M.	F.	N.
N.	λελυμένος	λελυμένη	λελυμένον
G. & A.	λελυμένου	λελυμένης	λελυμένου
D., L., & I.	λελυμένῳ	λελυμένῃ	λελυμένῳ
A.	λελυμένον	λελυμένην	λελυμένον

Plural

	M.	F.	N.
N.	λελυμένοι	λελυμέναι	λελυμένα
G. & A.	λελυμένων	λελυμένων	λελυμένων
D., L., & I.	λελυμένοις	λελυμέναις	λελυμένοις
A.	λελυμένους	λελυμένας	λελυμένα

5. The perfect infinitives of λύω are:

Active: λελυκέναι, to have loosed
Middle: λελύσθαι, to have loosed for one's self
Passive: λελύσθαι, to have been loosed

101

6. Reduplication in the perfect tense.

The most striking thing about the perfect tense is the reduplicated stem. Ordinarily this reduplication consists of doubling the initial consonant and inserting an ε between the two. Thus the reduplicated stem of λύω is λελυ-; of γράφω it is γεγραφ-; of γίνομαι it is γεγον-, etc. This, however, is only one of the ways a verb stem may be reduplicated. Here are other ways frequently found:

Verb stems beginning with φ, θ, or χ are reduplicated with the smoother consonants π, τ, and κ respectively. θνήσκω becomes τέθνηκα, etc.

Verb stems beginning with a vowel lengthen the vowel to form reduplication. ἐλπίζω becomes ἤλπικα, etc.

Verb stems beginning with two consonants sometimes reduplicate by prefixing an ε like an augment in the aorist. Thus the perfect of γινώσκω is ἔγνωκα (γνω- stem).

The only safe way to learn the correct perfect form for a verb is to check the word in the vocabulary. The *fourth* principal part will be the perfect active stem.

7. The tense sign for the perfect tense is κ. There are a few perfects which do not use the κ and are called second perfects; for example the perfect of ἀκούω is ἀκήκοα; of γίνομαι it is γέγονα, etc. The κ is, however, the usual form.

There are frequent changes in the verb stem when it ends in a consonant. For instance, verb stems ending in τ, δ, or θ drop the consonant before the κ of the perfect — ἐλπίζω (stem ἐλπιδ-) becomes ἤλπικα. These changes are best learned by observation in vocabulary study.

8. The perfect is a primary tense, but because of its functional nature, it uses secondary personal endings. The endings are the same as those of the first aorist except in the third personal plural form where -κασι is more frequently found than -καν.

9. Close observation should be given to the accent system in the above paradigms. The irregular accent is frequently the most certain way of identifying a perfect tense form.

10. It should be noted that the perfect middle and passive forms employ no connecting vowel. To the stem (the *fifth* form in the vocabulary listing) the endings are added directly: λέλυμαι, λελύσθαι, λελυμένος, η, ον, etc.

(2) The perfect tense function:

The Greek perfect tense stands alone in its function; English has no corresponding tense adequate for expressing the significance involved. The English past tense translations "I have loosed" — λέλυκα, "I have been loosed" — λέλυμαι, etc., are accommodations only. They do not express the full force of the Greek perfect. This is the Greek tense of "completed action," i.e., it indicates a completed action with a resulting state of being. The primary emphasis is on the resulting state of being. Involved in the Greek perfect are three ideas: an action in *progress,* its coming to a point of *culmination,* its existing as a *completed result.* Thus it implies a process but looks upon the process as having reached a consummation and existing as a completed state. The real nature of the Greek perfect is seen in the passive voice better than in the active. Hence γέγραπται may be translated "it has been written," but it is better translated "it is written," in which sense it pictures an act in progress, the point of culmination, and the existing completed result — "it has been written and stands written." Likewise ἐγήγερται "he is risen," and χάριτί ἐστε σεσωσμένοι "by grace are you saved," etc. For fuller discussion of the significance of the perfect tense and the variety of its usage see Dana and Mantey's *A Manual Grammar of the Greek New Testament* and Robertson's *A Grammar of the Greek New Testament.*

Try the following drill for review:

Distinguish between the present and the aorist tense. Distinguish between the imperfect and the aorist tense. Distinguish between the perfect and the aorist tense. The aorist is the tense of simple past action; the perfect is the tense of "past action plus existing result."

(3) In the verb paradigm in the back of this book will be

found the pluperfect and future perfect passive tenses. These are genuine but rare verb forms in the Greek New Testament. The pluperfect is the "perfect of past time" and is translated "I had loosed," etc. The future perfect passive is the perfect passive of future time and is translated "I shall have been loosed," etc. Further study of the tenses is unnecessary here but should be made by the student when he confronts the construction in the Greek New Testament.

80. Practical Application

Translate the following sentences:

1. τὰ γεγραμμένα ἐν τῷ βιβλίῳ τοῦ νόμου ἐστὶν ἀγαθά. 2. ὁ προφήτης εὐηγγελίσατο λέγων ὅτι ἡ βασιλεία τῶν οὐρανῶν ἤγγικεν. 3. ἀκηκόαμεν τὴν ἀλήθειαν καὶ ἐγνώκαμεν ὅτι ἀπὸ τοῦ Θεοῦ ἐστίν. 4. γεγόνατε τὰ τέκνα τοῦ Θεοῦ. 5. χάριτί ἐστε σεσωσμένοι διὰ πίστεως. 6. ἐγὼ ἐλήλυθα ἐν τῷ ὀνόματι τοῦ πατρός μου καὶ ὑμεῖς οὐ δέχεσθέ με. 7. πεπιστεύκαμεν καὶ ἐγνώκαμεν ὅτι σὺ εἶ ὁ ἅγιος τοῦ Θεοῦ. 8. ταῦτα εἶπεν ὁ Ἰησοῦς πρὸς τοὺς πεπιστευκότας εἰς αὐτόν. 9. ἤδη τὸ πνεῦμα τὸ ἅγιον ἐλήλυθεν εἰς τὸν κόσμον. 10. οἱ βεβαπτισμένοι μαθηταί εἰσιν ἐν τῇ ἐκκλησίᾳ. 11. οἱ μαθηταὶ βεβαπτισμένοι συνῆλθον εἰς τὸν οἶκον. 12. διὰ τοῦ προφήτου γέγραπται ὅτι ὁ Χριστὸς ἐλεύσεται ἐν ταῖς ἡμέραις ταύταις. 13. ὁ Κύριος ἀπέθανεν, ἀλλὰ νῦν ἐγήγερται. 14. οἱ ἐξεληλυθότες ἐκ τοῦ σκότους εἰς τὸ φῶς ἔγνωκαν ὅτι ὁ Θεός ἐστιν ἀγάπη. 15. ὁ Ἰησοῦς ἀπεκτάνθη, γέγονε δὲ βασιλεὺς τοῦ κόσμου.

LESSON 26

THE SUBJUNCTIVE MOOD: CONDITIONAL SENTENCES

81. Lexical Sudy

δικαιοσύνη, ἡ, righteousness
εὐαγγελίζομαι, I preach the gospel
μαρτυρία, ἡ, witness, testimony
οἰκία, ἡ, house
παιδίον, τό, child

ἐάν (*used with the subj.*) if
εἰ (*used with the ind.*) if
ἵνα (*used with the subj.*) in
order that, that

82. Grammatical Study

(1) The forms of the subjunctive mood:

Except for some very rare occurrences in the perfect tense the subjunctive mood is used only in the present and the aorist in New Testament Greek. It is the most regular of all the moods, consisting of the tense stem desired plus the forms of the present subjunctive of εἰμί. English equivalents are not given in the following paradigms because of the difficulty of translating the subjunctive in the abstract. An abundance of contextual illustrations will be found in the discussion which follows:

1. The present subjunctive of εἰμί is:

ὦ	ὦμεν
ᾖς	ἦτε
ᾖ	ὦσι(ν)

2. The present active subjunctive of λύω is:

λύω	λύωμεν
λύῃς	λύητε
λύῃ	λύωσι(ν)

105

3. The first aorist active subjunctive of λύω is λύσω, etc.

4. The second aorist active subjunctive of λείπω is λίπω, etc.

5. The present middle and passive subjunctive of λύω is:

λύωμαι	λυώμεθα
λύῃ	λύησθε
λύηται	λύωνται

6. The first aorist middle subjunctive of λύω is λύσωμαι, etc.

7. The second aorist middle subjunctive of λείπω is λίπωμαι, etc.

8. The first aorist passive of λύω is:

λυθῶ	λυθῶμεν
λυθῇς	λυθῆτε
λυθῇ	λυθῶσι (ν)

9. Any second aorist passive will be the second aorist stem plus -ῶ, -ῇς, -ῇ, etc.

10. In the above paradigms note the following:

a. There is a long connecting vowel ω/η replacing the short one ο/ε of the indicative mood.

b. All subjunctive tenses have *primary* endings and there is *no augment* in the aorist. This is due to the fact that the *time* of action is lost outside of the indicative mood, and *kind* of action is the all important thing.

c. The irregular accent in the aorist passive is the result of the contraction of θε- with the long ω/η connecting vowel.

(2) The function of the subjunctive mood:

In grammatical study mood is defined as the affirmation of the relation of action to reality. Is the action actually taking place, or is it only potential? This question introduces the two basic moods in any language: the *real* and the *potential*. In New Testament Greek there are four true moods; one expresses real action (indicative), three express potential action (subjunctive, optative, and imperative). In other words, action which is viewed by the speaker as real is expressed by the indicative mood; action

106

which is viewed by the speaker as possible, contingent upon certain conditions, is expressed by one of the potential moods according to the distance which the action is removed from reality. Four English sentences illustrate this principle:

Indicative mood: *The child runs.* This expresses action which is really taking place.

Subjunctive mood: *If the child run,* he will escape. This expresses action which is not really taking place but which is objectively possible. The child has the ability to run. This of all the potential moods is nearest to reality.

Optative mood: *Oh, that the child would run!* This expresses action which is not really taking place but which is subjectively possible. It is one step further removed from reality than the subjunctive.

Imperative mood: *Run, child.* This expresses action which is not really taking place but which is volitionally possible, i.e., the action will result from the exertion of the will of one to produce action on the part of another. It is the furthest removed from the real action of the indicative mood.

In previous study it has been observed that two things are indicated in Greek tense: *time* of action and *kind* of action. Of these two only *kind* of action remains outside of the indicative mood. The time of action is, then, in the subjunctive, relative to that of the main verb. The kind of action finds its expression as linear in the present and punctiliar in the aorist. Thus ἐὰν λύω means "if I continue loosing," and ἐὰν λύσω means "if I loose in one act." Note the time relation in the following sentences:

(1) ἔρχομαι ἵνα εἴπω αὐτῷ. "I *come* that I *may* speak to him."
(2) ἦλθον ἵνα εἴπω αὐτῷ. "I *came* that I *might* speak to him."
(3) ἐλεύσομαι ἵνα εἴπω αὐτῷ. "I *shall come* that I *may* speak to him."

In all these sentences the aorist subjunctive indicates a single act of speaking; in one the act is in present time, in another it is in past time, in the third it is in future time. The present subjunctive in the three sentences would express an extended conversation in present, past, or future time.

An interesting variety of expression is possible in the subjunctive moods. The following are frequently found:

1. The *hortatory* subjunctive is the use of the first person plural to exhort others to join us in an action. ἔλθωμεν εἰς τὸν οἶκον. *"Let us go* into the house."

2. The *prohibitive* subjunctive is the use of the second person aorist subjunctive (never the present) to express a negative entreaty or command. εἰς πειρασμὸν μὴ εἰσενέγκῃς ἡμᾶς. *"Lead us not* into temptation."* This forbids the beginning of an act and may well be translated "Don't ever . . ." Prohibition of the continuance of an act already in progress is expressed by the present imperative.

3. The *deliberative* subjunctive is used to express a question which is either a mere rhetorical device expecting no answer at all or a real question which expects an answer in the imperative. τί εἴπω ὑμῖν; *"What shall I say* to you?" If an answer is expected at all, it will be in the imperative, e.g., "say this" or "say that" or some similar expression.

4. The subjunctive is used to express *emphatic* negation. In this construction it employs the double negative οὐ μή and is much stronger than the simple οὐ with the indicative. οὐ μὴ ἐκφύγωσιν. "They shall *by no means* escape."

5. The *final* subjunctive is the use of the subordinate clause to express purpose. The main particle used in this construction is ἵνα. ἔρχομαι ἵνα εἴπω αὐτῷ. "I come *in order that* I may speak to him."

6. *Probable future condition* is expressed by the subjunctive with ἐάν. See below, conditional sentence third class.

(3) Conditional Sentences:

In the Greek New Testament there are many kinds of conditional statements. There are four classes of conditional sentences which are outstanding in usage. They follow with their means of expression:

1. First class condition *affirms* the reality of the condition. It

is expressed by εἰ with the indicative mood in the protasis (if clause) and almost any mood or tense in the apodosis (main or fulfilment clause). εἰ μαθηταί ἐσμεν τοῦ Κυρίου σωθησόμεθα. "If we are disciples of the Lord, we shall be saved." This construction confirms the condition and is best translated "since we are, etc."

2. Second class condition is *contrary to fact* condition. This is to many one of the most baffling constructions in the English language where it is expressed by the subjunctive mood. In Greek it is expressed by the secondary tenses of the indicative mood. The correct form is εἰ with the indicative in the protasis and ἄν with the indicative in the apodosis. εἰ ἦς ὧδε οὐκ ἄν ἀπέθανεν ὁ ἀδελφός μου. "If you *had been here,* my brother *would not have died."* The fact is "You were not here and hence my brother died." Study these English sentences in contrary to fact condition:

> If I were you, I would not go.
> If you were older, you would understand.
> If this were Sunday, I would be at church.
> If he had left yesterday, he would be here today.
> I wish my father were here.

Study these English sentences which are real conditions:

> If he was sick, he did not show it.
> If he was there, I did not see him.
> If the pen was new, why did it not write?
> If he was mayor, I can understand his action.

3. Third class condition is the *probable future* condition. It is expressed by ἐάν with the subjunctive in the protasis and any form needed in the apodosis. It expresses that which is not really taking place but which probably will take place in the future. τοῦτο ποιήσομεν ἐὰν ἐπιτρέπῃ ὁ Θεός. "This we will do *if God permit."* That is, we are not now doing it, but it is probable that we will do it on the condition of God's permitting us.

4. Fourth class condition is the *possible future* condition. It is expressed by εἰ with the optative mood in the protasis and ἄν with the optative mood in the apodosis. No example of the fully

written construction is found in the New Testament. The words in parenthesis are supplied in the following illustration. ἀλλ' εἰ καὶ πάσχοιτε διὰ δικαιοσύνην, μακάροι (ἄν εἴητε). "But even *if you should* suffer for righteousness' sake, *you would be* happy." In other words, you are not now suffering for righteousness' sake, and, while it is possible, it is improbable that you will. This construction is expressive of that which is not now a reality and has little prospect of becoming a reality.

Study the following English sentences in the light of the above classification:

First class: If he is studying, he will learn the Greek.
Second class: If he had studied, he would have learned the Greek.
Third class: If he studies, he will learn the Greek.
Fourth class: If he would study, he would learn the Greek.

83. Practical Application:

Translate the following sentences:

1. ἐὰν εἴπωμεν ὅτι ἁμαρτίαν οὐκ ἔχομεν, ἡ ἀλήθεια οὐκ ἔστιν ἐν ἡμῖν. 2. εἰσήλθομεν εἰς τὴν ἐκκλησίαν ἵνα ἀκούσωμεν τὸν λόγον τοῦ Θεοῦ τὸν κηρυσσόμενον. 3. εἰ αὕτη ἐστὶν ἡ μαρτυρία τοῦ ἰδόντος τὸν Κύριον πιστεύω αὐτήν. 4. ἀκούω τὸν λόγον αὐτοῦ ἵνα γινώσκω τὸ θέλημα αὐτοῦ. 5. εὐαγγελιζώμεθα ἵνα τὰ τέκνα ἀκούσῃ καὶ πιστεύῃ. 6. ἐὰν εἴπωμεν ὅτι κοινωνίαν ἔχομεν μετ' αὐτοῦ καὶ μένωμεν ἐν ἁμαρτίᾳ, ψευδόμεθα. 7. οἱ μὴ πιστεύοντες τὸ εὐαγγέλιον οὐ μὴ σωθῶσιν ἐν τῇ δυνάμει αὐτοῦ 8. μένωμεν ἐν ἁμαρτίᾳ ἵνα ἡ δύναμις τῆς χάριτος τοῦ Θεοῦ βλέπηται; 9. εἰ ἐκήρυξας τὸ εὐαγγέλιον, οἱ ἄν ἁμαρτωλοὶ ἐπίστευσαν. 10. ἐὰν εἰσέλθητε εἰς τὴν οἰκίαν τοῦ μαθητοῦ, διδάξει ὑμῖν τοὺς λόγους τῆς ζωῆς. 11. ὁ υἱὸς τοῦ ἀνθρώπου ἦλθεν ἵνα σώσῃ ἀνθρώπους ἀπὸ τῶν ἁμαρτιῶν αὐτῶν. 12. μὴ εἰσέλθῃς εἰς τοὺς οἴκους τῶν πονηρῶν.

110

LESSON 27

THE IMPERATIVE MOOD

84. Lexical Study

ἁγιάζω, I sanctify   πίνω, I drink

θέλω, I wish   σπείρω, I sow

οὖς, ὠτός, τό, ear   ἄχρι, (*with gen.*) until

                                  πρίν, before

85. Grammatical Study

(1) The forms of the imperative mood:

The imperative mood appears in the New Testament in the present and aorist tenses. There is no first person in the imperative mood; there is a third person which has no English parallel and must be translated with the permissive idea "let him . . ." etc. There are some variant forms for the third person plural. In this study only the usual forms will be learned; the variant forms may be observed when they appear in the study of the Greek New Testament. There is, of course, no augment in the aorist forms. English equivalents are not given in the paradigms; they are well illustrated in the discussion which follows.

1. The present active imperative of λύω is:

     2nd person λῦε   λύετε

     3rd person λυέτω   λυέτωσαν

2. The present middle and passive imperative of λύω is:

     2nd person λύου   λύεσθε

     3rd person λυέσθω   λυέσθωσαν

111

3. The first aorist active imperative of λύω is:

    2nd person λῦσον   λύσατε
    3rd person λυσάτω   λυσάτωσαν

4. The first aorist middle imperative of λύω is:

    2nd person λῦσαι   λύσασθε
    3rd person λυσάσθω   λυσάσθωσαν

5. The first aorist passive imperative of λύω is:

    2nd person λύθητι   λύθητε
    3rd person λυθήτω   λυθήτωσαν

6. The second aorist active imperative of λείπω is:

    2nd person λίπε   λίπετε
    3rd person λιπέτω   λιπέτωσαν

7. The second aorist passive imperative of ἀποστέλλω is:

    2nd person ἀποστάληθι   ἀποστάλητε
    3rd person ἀποσταλήτω   ἀποσταλήτωσαν

8. The present imperative of εἰμι is:

    2nd person ἴσθι   ἔστε
    3rd person ἔστω   ἔστωσαν

(2) The function of the imperative:

The basic function of the imperative mood has been noted in paragraph 82 (2). It is the mood which expresses action which is to be realized by the exercise of the will of one person upon that of another. Thus λῦε τὸν ἄνθρωπον means "loose the man"; λυέτω τὸν ἄνθρωπον means "let him loose the man," etc.

The *time* of action is lost in the imperative mood. The distinction between present and aorist in the imperative mood is to be found in *kind* of action. The present imperative has to do with action which is in progress: λῦε αὐτόν, "continue loosing him"; the aorist imperative has to do with action which has not yet started: λῦσον αὐτόν, "loose him," i.e., "start loosing him." It is the usual difference between linear and punctiliar action with a slight change of emphasis due to the nature of the imperative.

The following are the basic uses of the imperative:

1. Cohortative — positive command. The illustrations in the last paragraph are sufficient here. Either the present or the aorist imperative may be used.

2. Prohibitive — negative command. Only the present imperative is used in this construction. The negative particle μή is to be used, and the construction prohibits the continuance of an act which is in progress. It may well be translated "Stop . . ." μὴ λῦε αὐτόν. "Stop loosing him." μὴ λέγετε ταῦτα. "Stop saying these things." Compare this with the aorist subjunctive used to prohibit the beginning of an action, paragraph 82, (2), b. This distinction is of tremendous importance.

3. Entreaty. This is the use of the imperative to express a request rather than a direct command. A good example is found in the prayer of Jesus in John 17:11: πάτερ ἅγιε, τήρησον αὐτοὺς ἐν τῷ ὀνόματί σου. "Holy Father, keep them in thy name."

4. Permissive. This is the use of the third person imperative and needs the English auxiliary verb "let" to make its meaning clear. λυέτω τὸν ἄνθρωπον. "Let him continue loosing the man." λυσάτω τὸν ἄνθρωπον. "Let him loose (or start loosing) the man," etc.

86. Practical application

Translate the following sentences:

1. ἁγίαζε τὸ ἱερὸν τοῦ Θεοῦ. 2. ἀκούσατε τὸν λόγον τοῦ Κυρίου καὶ σώθητε. 3. μὴ λέγε πονηρὰ τοῖς τέκνοις καὶ εἶπε ἀγαθὰ αὐτοῖς. 4. ἀκουέσθωσαν αἱ ,παραβολαὶ περὶ τῆς βασιλείας ἐν τῇ ἐκκλησίᾳ. 5. Κύριε, κατάβηθι πρίν ἀποθανεῖν τὸ παιδίον μου. 6. εἰ ὁ ἄνθρωπος πιστεύει εἰς τὸν Κύριον, βαπτισθήτω. 7. πίνετε τὸ ὕδωρ τῆς ζωῆς καὶ ἐσθίετε τὸν ἄρτον τῆς ζωῆς. 8. γίνου πιστὸς ἄχρι θανάτου. 9. ὁ ἔχων ὦτα ἀκουσάτω. 10. μὴ εἰσέλθῃς εἰς τὴν πόλιν τὴν οὖσαν ἐν τῷ ὄρει. 11. ἴδετε τὰς χεῖράς μου. 12. λαβὼν αὐτὸν ἄγε αὐτὸν πρὸς ἡμᾶς.

LESSON 28

CONTRACT VERBS

87. Lexical Study

ἀγαπάω, I love (to put
    supreme value on)
δηλόω, I show
εὐλογέω, I bless
εὐχαριστέω, I give thanks
ζητέω, I seek
θεωρέω, I behold
καλέω, I call
λαλέω, I speak

παρακαλέω, I exhort, I
    comfort
περιπατέω, I walk about
ποιέω, I do, I make
σταυρόω, I crucify
τηρέω, I keep
τιμάω, I honor
φιλέω, I love (to have a
    warm personal
    affection for)

88. Grammatical Study

(1) Contract verbs form a special class of ω verbs. These are verbs with the stem ending in -αω, -οω, and -εω. This vowel (a, o, or ε) contracts with the connecting vowel ο/ε in the present system to form a single long vowel or diphthong. This contraction takes place in *all forms* of the present and imperfect tenses. Because of tense sign consonants this contraction does not take place in aorist, future, perfect, pluperfect, and future perfect passive tenses. These tenses are regular except for the lengthening of the stem vowel (a, o, or ε) before the σ, κ, etc. Check this in the principal parts of the verbs in the above vocabulary. Note that καλέω is an exception to this rule; the future is καλέσω rather than καλήσω, etc.

114

(2) The following chart indicates the regular contractions of stem vowels (vertical column) with connecting vowel, etc. (top line). $\epsilon + \epsilon = \epsilon\iota$, $\epsilon + \eta = \eta$, etc.

	ε	η	ει	ῃ	ο	ω	ου	οι
ε	ει	η	ει	ῃ	ου	ω	ου	οι
α	α	α	ᾳ	ᾳ	ω	ω	ω	ῳ
ο	ου	ω	οι	οι	ου	ω	ου	οι

(3) The following principles indicate the reasons for the above contractions:

1. Vowel contracting with vowel

   a. Two *like* vowels form the common long vowel:
   $a + a = a$, $\epsilon + \eta = \eta$, etc.
   Except: $\epsilon + \epsilon = \epsilon\iota$, and $o + o = ov$.

   b. An o-sound vowel (o or ω) overcomes a, ϵ, or η (whether in first or second position) and forms ω.
   Except: $\epsilon + o = ov$, and $o + \epsilon = ov$.

   c. When a- and ϵ- (or η) contract, the one which comes first overcomes the other and forms its long.
   $a + \epsilon = a$, $a + \eta = a$, $\epsilon + a = \eta$.

2. Vowel contracting with diphthong

   a. A vowel disappears before a diphthong which begins with the same vowel.
   $\epsilon + \epsilon\iota = \epsilon\iota$, $o + ov = ov$.

   b. When a vowel comes before a diphthong which does not begin with the same vowel, it is contracted with the diphthong's first vowel, and the diphthong's second vowel disappears unless it is ι in which case it becomes subscript.
   $a + \epsilon\iota = ᾳ$, $a + ov = ω$, $\epsilon + ov = ov$.
   Except: $o + \epsilon\iota = οι$, $o + \eta = οι$, $\epsilon + οι = οι$.

   There are two unusual exceptions to this rule. The present active infinitive of verbs ending in -αω has

115

âν rather than -ᾷν, which would be regular. The present active infinitive of verbs ending in -οω has -οῦν rather than -οιν, which would be regular.

(4) Four things should be noted regarding accents in contract verbs.

1. The accent on the uncontracted form will be recessive just as it will in any other verb.

2. If the accent appeared on one of the vowels suffering contraction, it will appear on the resulting contracted form.

τιμάω = τιμῶ, but ἐτίμαον = ἐτίμων

3. If it appeared on the first of the two, the resulting contracted form will be circumflex, τιμάω = τιμῶ.

4. If it appeared on the second of the two, the resulting contracting form will have an acute accent, τιμαόμεθα = τιμώμεθα.

(5) The present active indicative of τιμάω follows. It should be understood that the uncontracted forms do not appear in the New Testament; they are included to show how the correct contracted form is constructed.

τιμάω = τιμῶ	τιμάομεν = τιμῶμεν
τιμάεις = τιμᾷς	τιμάετε = τιμᾶτε
τιμάει = τιμᾷ	τιμάουσι = τιμῶσι

Any present or imperfect form of a verb ending in -αω may be found by adding the regular required ending to the verb stem and then forming the contraction. The student should drill on this and check his results with the verb chart in the paradigms in the back of the book.

(6) The present active indicative of φιλέω and δηλόω follow:

φιλέω = φιλῶ	δηλόω = δηλῶ
φιλέεις = φιλεῖς	δηλόεις = δηλοῖς
φιλέει = φιλεῖ	δηλόει = δηλοῖ
φιλέομεν = φιλοῦμεν	δηλόομεν = δηλοῦμεν
φιλέετε = φιλεῖτε	δηλόετε = δηλοῦτε
φιλέουσι = φιλοῦσι	δηλόουσι = δηλοῦσι

The drill suggested for learning the forms of τιμάω should be applied with these verbs.

(7) Liquid verbs (those with the stem ending in λ, μ, ν, ρ) drop the σ in the future, add an ε, and then form regular contraction. Thus the future active indicative of κρίνω, "I judge," will not be κρίνσω, etc. but κρινῶ, κρινεῖς, κρινεῖ, etc. See paragraph 49 (3).

89. Practical Application

Translate the following sentences:

1. εἰ ἀγαπῶμεν τὸν Κύριον, τηρῶμεν τὰς ἐντολὰς αὐτοῦ καὶ ποιῶμεν τὰ λαλούμενα ἡμῖν ὑπ' αὐτοῦ. 2. ἐζήτουν αὐτὸν οἱ πονηροὶ, ἵνα θεωρῶσι τὰ ποιούμενα ὑπ' αὐτοῦ. 3. ὁ μαθητὴς ἐλάλησεν ταῦτα τοῖς περιπατοῦσιν ἐν τῷ ἱερῷ. 4. οὐκ εὐλογήσει ὁ Θεὸς τὸν μὴ περιπατοῦντα κατὰ τὰς ἐντολὰς τοῦ υἱοῦ αὐτοῦ. 5. ταῦτα ἐποιεῖτε ἡμῖν ὅτι φιλεῖτε τὸν καλέσαντα ὑμᾶς εἰς τὴν βασιλείαν αὐτοῦ. 6. ἐθεώρουν τὸν Ἰησοῦν σταυρούμενον ὑπὸ τῶν στρατιωτῶν. 7. εὐχαριστῶμεν τῷ Θεῷ καὶ τιμῶμεν τὸ ὄνομα αὐτοῦ. 8. ὁ Θεὸς ἠγάπησεν τὸν κόσμον καὶ παρακαλεῖ ἀνθρώπους ἀγαπᾶν τὸν υἱὸν αὐτοῦ. 9. ὁ Ἰησοῦς λέγει τῷ μαθητῇ, Σίμων, φιλεῖς με; 10. καὶ εἶπεν αὐτῷ, Κύριε, σὺ γινώσκεις ὅτι φιλῶ σε. 11. ἐὰν ἐν τῷ φωτὶ περιπατῶμεν ὡς αὐτός ἐστιν ἐν τῷ φωτί, τὸ αἷμα Ἰησοῦ τοῦ υἱοῦ αὐτοῦ καθαρίζει ἡμᾶς ἀπὸ τῆς ἁμαρτίας ἡμῶν. 12. ἐὰν εἴπωμεν ὅτι οὐχ ἡμαρτήκαμεν, ψεύστην ποιοῦμεν αὐτὸν καὶ ὁ λόγος αὐτοῦ οὐκ ἔστιν ἐν ἡμῖν.

117

LESSON 29

PRONOUNS

90. Lexical Study

Review the inflection of the five pronouns already learned:
(1) First person, ἐγώ, I
(2) Second person, σύ, you
(3) Third person, αὐτός, αὐτή, αὐτό, he, she, it
(4) Near demonstrative, οὗτος, αὕτη, τοῦτο, this
(5) Remote demonstrative, ἐκεῖνος, ἐκείνη, ἐκεῖνο, that

91. Grammatical Study

(1) The relative pronoun, ὅς, who, which, that

	Singular			Plural		
	M.	F.	N.	M.	F.	N.
N.	ὅς	ἥ	ὅ	οἵ	αἵ	ἅ
G. & A.	οὗ	ἧς	οὗ	ὧν	ὧν	ὧν
D., L., & I.	ᾧ	ᾗ	ᾧ	οἷς	αἷς	οἷς
A.	ὅν	ἥν	ὅ	οὕς	ἅς	ἅ

The relative pronoun is used to relate one substantive to another. It agrees with its antecedent in gender and number, but its case is determined by its function in its clause. Compare the case function of the relative pronoun in these sentences: (1) ὁ ἄνθρωπος ὃς εἶδε τὸν Κύριόν ἐστιν νῦν ἀπόστολος. (2) ὁ ἄνθρωπος ὃν εἶδες ἐξῆλθεν ἐκ τῆς πόλεως.

Frequently a relative pronoun is so closely related to its antecedent that it is attracted to the case of its antecedent, i.e., it takes the case form of the antecedent even though it retains its own case function. For example: ὃς ἂν πίῃ ἐκ τοῦ ὕδατος οὗ ἐγὼ δώσω αὐτῷ — "whoever drinks of the water *which* I shall give him." The relative οὗ is grammatically the direct object of δώσω, and it is expected to be in the accusative case. It has been *attracted* to the case form of its antecedent. This is an example of the use of the conditional relative — one of the uses of the third class conditional sentence. The relative with ἄν or ἐάν and the subjunctive is used to express clauses which in English would be expressed by these words: whoever, whichever, whatever, whenever, wherever, etc.

Frequently the antecedent of a relative pronoun is not expressed. ὃς οὐκ ἔστιν καθ᾽ ὑμῶν ὑπὲρ ὑμῶν ἐστιν. This is best translated: "*He who* is not against you is for you."

(2) The interrogative pronoun, τίς, who? what?

	Singular		Plural	
	M. & F.	N.	M. & F.	N.
N.	τίς	τί	τίνες	τίνα
G. & A.	τίνος	τίνος	τίνων	τίνων
D., L., & I.	τίνι	τίνι	τίσι(ν)	τίσι(ν)
A.	τίνα	τί	τίνας	τίνα

This is used to introduce direct or indirect questions. τίς εἶ; "Who are you?" τί λέγει; "What is he saying?" οὐ τί ἐγὼ θέλω, ἀλλὰ τί σύ — "not what I wish but what thou wishest." οἶδά σε τίς εἶ. "I know you who you are." Note: The *acute* accent in the *interrogative* pronoun is *never* changed to the *grave*.

(3) The indefinite pronoun, τις, τι

The forms of the indefinite pronoun are the same as those of the interrogative except that the indefinite pronoun is enclitic, i.e., it will be accented only when the rules for the accent of enclitics apply.

The function of the indefinite pronoun is indicated in such expressions as: someone, somebody, something, a certain one, a certain thing. ἐὰν μή τις γεννηθῇ ἄνωθεν — "except somebody [that is,

119

'anybody'] be born from above . . ." εἰς τὴν ἐκκλησίαν εἰσῆλθέ τις. "Into the church came a certain man."

(4) The indefinite relative pronoun, ὅστις, who.

This pronoun is so named because it is a combination of the relative ὅς and the indefinite τις. In form it appears only in the nominative case in the New Testament: singular ὅστις, ἥτις, ὅτι, and plural οἵτινες, αἵτινες, ἅτινα.

In function it is qualitative in nature. It is usually translated by the simple "who," but its meaning is far more than that. The expression "who is of such nature" is a good translation of the idea. See Romans 1:25: οἵτινες μετήλλαξαν τὴν ἀλήθειαν τοῦ Θεοῦ ἐν τῷ ψεύδει, etc. — "who were of such nature that they exchanged the truth of God for a lie, etc." Always look for the qualitative idea in this word.

(5) The reciprocal pronoun ἀλλήλων, each other.

This appears in only three case forms in the New Testament ἀλλήλων, ἀλλήλοις, ἀλλήλους. In function it represents an interchange of action between the members of a plural subject. ἀγαπῶμεν ἀλλήλους. "Let us love one another." ἐξεκαύθησαν ἐν τῇ ὀρέξει αὐτῶν εἰς ἀλλήλους. "They burned in their lust for one another."

(6) The reflexive pronouns

First Person, myself

	Singular		Plural	
	Masc.	Fem.	Masc.	Fem.
G., A.	ἐμαυτοῦ	ἐμαυτῆς	ἑαυτῶν	ἑαυτῶν
D., L., I.	ἐμαυτῷ	ἐμαυτῇ	ἑαυτοῖς	ἑαυταῖς
A.	ἐμαυτόν	ἐμαυτήν	ἑαυτούς	ἑαυτάς

Second Person, yourself

	Masc.	Fem.	Masc.	Fem.
G., A.	σεαυτοῦ	σεαυτῆς	ἑαυτῶν	ἑαυτῶν
D., L., I.	σεαυτῷ	σεαυτῇ	ἑαυτοῖς	ἑαυταῖς
A.	σεαυτόν	σεαυτήν	ἑαυτούς	ἑαυτάς

120

Third Person, himself, etc.

	Masc.	Fem.	Neu.	Masc.	Fem.	Neu.
G., A.	ἑαυτοῦ	ἑαυτῆς	ἑαυτοῦ	ἑαυτῶν	ἑαυτῶν	ἑαυτῶν
D., L., I.	ἑαυτῷ	ἑαυτῇ	ἑαυτῷ	ἑαυτοῖς	ἑαυταῖς	ἑαυτοῖς
A.	ἑαυτόν	ἑαυτήν	ἑαυτό	ἑαυτούς	ἑαυτάς	ἑαυτά

Observe the absence of the nominative form in these paradigms. The reflexive idea can be expressed only in the oblique cases. The intensive "myself," "yourself," "himself," etc., in the nominative are cared for by the use of the intensive αὐτός. αὐτὸς ἐγὼ λέγω — "I myself say," etc.

Observe, too, that the plural forms for the third person reflexive are also used for the first and second persons. The old first and second person plural forms were dropped by the Greeks.

The function of the pronoun is regular in every way. It expresses the action of the subject upon itself. οὐ γὰρ ἑαυτοὺς κηρύσσομεν. "For we preach not ourselves." λέγω ταῦτα περὶ ἐμαυτοῦ. "I say these things concerning myself."

(7) The possessive pronouns (or adjectives)

First Person, ἐμός, my

		Singular			Plural	
	Masc.	Fem.	Neu.	Masc.	Fem.	Neu.
N.	ἐμός	ἐμή	ἐμόν	ἐμοί	ἐμαί	ἐμά
G., A.	ἐμοῦ	ἐμῆς	ἐμοῦ	ἐμῶν	ἐμῶν	ἐμῶν
D., L., I.	ἐμῷ	ἐμῇ	ἐμῷ	ἐμοῖς	ἐμαῖς	ἐμοῖς
A.	ἐμόν	ἐμήν	ἐμόν	ἐμούς	ἐμάς	ἐμά

Like ἐμός are declined σός, σή, σόν, second person; and, with the change noted in the feminine, ἴδιος, ἰδία, ἴδιον, third person; ἡμέτερος, -α, -ον, first plural; ὑμέτερος, -α, -ον, second plural.

These are sometimes classified as possessive adjectives since they agree in gender, number, and case with the noun they modify. Note the following usage. The same agreement will maintain in any case construction.

121

ὁ ἐμὸς οἶκος	— my house	οἱ ἐμοὶ οἶκοι	— my houses
ὁ σὸς οἶκος	— your house	οἱ σοὶ οἶκοι	— your houses
ὁ ἴδιος οἶκος	— his house	οἱ ἴδιοι οἶκοι	— his houses
ὁ ἡμέτερος οἶκος	— our house	οἱ ἡμέτεροι οἶκοι	— our houses
ὁ ὑμέτερος οἶκος	— your house	οἱ ὑμέτεροι οἶκοι	— your houses

(8) The negative pronouns

οὐδείς, no one, usually with indicative mood.
μηδείς, no one, usually with moods other than indicative.

	Masc.	Fem.	Neu.
N.	οὐδείς	οὐδεμία	οὐδέν
G., A.	οὐδενός	οὐδεμιᾶς	οὐδενός
D., L., I.	οὐδενί	οὐδεμιᾷ	οὐδενί
A.	οὐδένα	οὐδεμίαν	οὐδέν

μηδείς is declined the same way; obviously there is no plural for either word. This is in reality the declension of the numeral "one," εἷς, μία, ἕν in combination with the negative particles οὐδέ and μηδέ. The following illustrations introduce the function of this pronoun: (1) οὐδεὶς ἔρχεται πρὸς τὸν πατέρα εἰ μὴ δι' ἐμοῦ. "No one comes to the Father except [if not] through me." (2) μηδεὶς πλανάτω ὑμᾶς. "Let no one deceive you."

92. Practical Application

Translate 1 John 1:5-10. If there are words which have not appeared in vocabulary study up to here, check them in the vocabulary in the back of the grammar or in another lexicon.

LESSON 30

ADJECTIVES

93. Lexical Study

ἀληθής, ἀληθές, true
μέγας, μεγάλη, μέγα, great
πᾶς, πᾶσα, πᾶν, every
πολύς, πολλή, πολύ, much, many

94. Grammatical Study

The following are examples of adjectives which do not follow the regular pattern previously studied. Some of these follow the second declension in masculine and neuter and the first declension in the feminine but have some short forms (μέγας and πολύς). One follows the third declension in masculine and neuter and the first declension in the feminine (πᾶς). The other one (ἀληθής) follows the third declension all the way but has only two forms, one for masculine and feminine and another for neuter. There are many other "third declension" adjectives which will be observed in the study of the New Testament. Those in this lesson are representative and much used.

(1) The declension of πᾶς, πᾶσα, πᾶν, all

	Singular			Plural		
	Masc.	Fem.	Neu.	Masc.	Fem.	Neu.
N.	πᾶς	πᾶσα	πᾶν	πάντες	πᾶσαι	πάντα
G., A.	παντός	πάσης	παντός	πάντων	πασῶν	πάντων
D., L., I.	παντί	πάσῃ	παντί	πᾶσι(ν)	πάσαις	πᾶσι(ν)
A.	πάντα	πᾶσαν	πᾶν	πάντας	πάσας	πάντα

123

The stem vowel α is short except where compensation has taken place because of some loss. The usage is varied:

1. Predicate position with a noun: πᾶσα ἡ πόλις — "all the city."
2. Attributive position with a noun: ἡ πᾶσα πόλις — "the whole city."
3. With a singular anarthrous noun: πᾶσα πόλις — "every city."
4. Predicate position with a participle: πᾶς ὁ πιστεύων — "everyone who believes."

(2) The declension of μέγας, μεγάλη, μέγα, great

		Singular			Plural	
	Masc.	Fem.	Neu.	Masc.	Fem.	Neu.
N.	μέγας	μεγάλη	μέγα	μεγάλοι	μεγάλαι	μεγάλα
G., A.	μεγάλου	μεγάλης	μεγάλου	μεγάλων	μεγάλων	μεγάλων
D., L., I.	μεγάλῳ	μεγάλῃ	μεγάλῳ	μεγάλοις	μεγάλαις	μεγάλοις
A.	μέγαν	μεγάλην	μέγα	μεγάλους	μεγάλας	μεγάλα

(3) The declension of πολύς, πολλή, πολύ, much

		Singular			Plural	
	Masc.	Fem.	Neu.	Masc.	Fem.	Neu.
N.	πολύς	πολλή	πολύ	πολλοί	πολλαί	πολλά
G., A.	πολλοῦ	πολλῆς	πολλοῦ	πολλῶν	πολλῶν	πολλῶν
D., L., I.	πολλῷ	πολλῇ	πολλῷ	πολλοῖς	πολλαῖς	πολλοῖς
A.	πολύν	πολλήν	πολύ	πολλούς	πολλάς	πολλά

(4) The declension of ἀληθής, ἀληθές, true

		Singular		Plural	
	Masc. & Fem.	Neu.	Masc. & Fem.	Neu.
N.	ἀληθής	ἀληθές	ἀληθεῖς	ἀληθῆ
G., A.	ἀληθοῦς	ἀληθοῦς	ἀληθῶν	ἀληθῶν
D., L., I.	ἀληθεῖ	ἀληθεῖ	ἀληθέσι (ν)	ἀληθέσι (ν)
A.	ἀληθῆ	ἀληθές	ἀληθεῖς	ἀληθῆ

The stem is ἀληθεσ-. In most of the forms the final σ is dropped and the stem vowel ε contracts with the ending. This explains the unusual accent.

(5) Comparison of adjectives. Adjectives in Greek have three degrees: positive, comparative, and superlative. When the adjective is regular in comparison, the following forms will be used: Comparative -τερος, -α, -ον declined like a regular adjective of the first and second declensions. Superlative -τατος, -η, -ον or -ιστος, -η, -ον like a regular adjective of the first and second declensions. Observe: ἰσχυρός, -α, -ον— "strong"; ἰσχυρότερος, -α, -ον—"stronger"; ἰσχυρότατος, -η, -ον—"strongest." Superlative forms are rare; the superlative idea is frequently expressed by the comparative form.

When the adjective is irregular in comparison, the stem of the word is changed. Example: μικρός — "little"; ἐλάσσω — "less"; ἐλάχιστος — "least." These must be learned as a part of the lexical study when they appear in the New Testament.

(6) There is no systematic treatment for adverbs. Some are formed from the genitive neuter plural adjective substituting ς for ν. Example: καλός — "good"; genitive plural, καλῶν; adverb, καλῶς — "well." Others are so diverse that they are best learned as they appear in usage in the expression of ideas of temporal, local, or other significance; "how long?", "when?", "where?", etc.

95. Practical Application

Translate 1 John 2:1-6.

LESSON 31

VERBS OF THE -μι CONJUGATION

96. Lexical Study

δίδωμι, δώσω, ἔδωκα, δέδωκα, δέδομαι, ἐδόθην, I give

ἵστημι, στήσω, ἔστησα (ἔστην), ἔστηκα, ἔσταμαι, ἐστάθην, I stand

τίθημι, θήσω, ἔθηκα, τέθεικα, τέθειμαι, ἐτέθην, I place, I put

97. Grammatical Study

The verbs of this conjugation differ from ω verbs only in the present, imperfect, and second aorist. A study of the principal parts of the verbs above indicates the similarity of future, first aorist, perfect, and aorist passive to verbs studied up to here.

The characteristic mark of this conjugation is the reduplication of the stem in the present tense using ι rather than ε which is used in the perfect. The stem of δίδωμι is -δο-, of ἵστημι it is -στα-, and of τίθημι it is -θε-. Note that an original σίστημι has become ἵστημι in general usage. The short stem vowel is lengthened in some forms.

Use the following analysis as an aid in studying the verb paradigms in the back of the book. The primary active endings are: -μι, -ς, -τι (or -σι), -μεν, -τε, -ασι.

A. Indicative Mood

I. δίδωμι (stem -δο-)

1. Present tense:

   (1) Stem reduplicated with ι.
   (2) Active voice uses long stem vowel ω in singular; o in plural.

126

(3) Middle and passive use short stem vowel ɔ all the way.

2. Imperfect tense:

    (1) Stem reduplicated as in present.
    (2) Active voice uses long stem vowel ου in singular; ο in plural.
    (3) Middle and passive use short stem vowel ο all the way.

3. Aorist tense:

    (1) Active voice has regular first aorist ἔδωκα.
    (2) Middle voice has regular second aorist ἐδόμην.
    (3) Passive voice has regular first aorist ἐδόθην.

II. ἵστημι (stem -στα-)

1. Present tense:

    (1) Reduplication with ι and rough breathing mark.
    (2) Active voice uses long stem vowel η in singular; α in plural.
    (3) Middle and passive use short stem vowel α all the way.

2. Imperfect tense:

    (1) Reduplication as in present.
    (2) Active voice uses stem vowel as present.
    (3) Middle and passive use stem vowel as present.

3. Aorist tense:

    (1) Active voice has a regular first aorist ἔστησα and a regular second aorist ἔστην.
    (2) Middle forms do not appear in the New Testament.
    (3) Passive voice has a regular first aorist.

III. τίθημι (stem -θε-)

1. Present tense:

    (1) Reduplicates with ι and τ rather than θ.
    (2) Active voice uses long stem vowel η in singular; ε in plural.
    (3) Middle and passive voice use short stem vowel all the way.

2. Imperfect tense:
   (1) Reduplicates as present tense.
   (2) Active voice uses long stem vowel η/ει in singular; ε in plural.
   (3) Middle and passive use short stem vowel ε all the way.
3. Aorist tense:
   (1) Active voice has regular first aorist ἔθηκα.
   (2) Middle voice has regular second aorist ἐθέμην.
   (3) Passive voice has regular first aorist ἐτέθην instead of ἐθέθην.

B. Subjunctive Mood

These verbs form their subjunctive in the regular way.

1. Present tense:
   (1) Stem reduplicates as in indicative mood.
   (2) Long stem vowels are used all the way.
   (3) Regular subjunctive endings of ω verb are used.
   (4) Contraction occurs between stem vowel and connecting vowel ω/η or ending.

2. Aorist tense:
   (1) Active and middle follow second aorist; passive follows first aorist.
   (2) Active and middle use long stem vowel; passive uses short stem vowel.
   (3) Contraction occurs between stem vowel and connecting vowel ω/η or ending.

μι verb forms other than the above tenses and moods are regular enough to be recognized when they appear in use. The student should learn well the present and second aorist systems of the above verbs. There are many other μι verbs which are so irregular and infrequent that it appears wise to omit them for beginners.

98. Practical Application

Translate 1 John 2:7-11.

LESSON 32

THE ARTICLE

99. Lexical Study

ἀλαζονία, ἡ, vainglory
ἀφίημι, I forgive
βίος, ὁ, life (compare with
  ζωή and ψυχή in lexi-
  con)

ἔγνωκα, I have known
  (perfect active of
  γινώσκω)
νεανίσκος, ὁ, a young man
νικάω, I overcome, I conquer

100. Grammatical Study

The Greek had no indefinite article. The words τις and εἷς many times are close to the English use of the indefinite article "a" or "an." The Greek definite article ὁ, ἡ, τό was much used and is of tremendous importance in the interpretation of the New Testament. In all probability it was originally a demonstrative pronoun; it retains that force frequently in the New Testament.

The basic function of the Greek article is to identify. At this point an important differentiation should be observed. When the article is used with a construction, the thing emphasized is "identity"; when the article is not used, the thing emphasized is quality of character. ὁ νόμος means "the law." It points out a particular law and gives specific identity. νόμος means "law" in general. When Paul says in Romans 3:21, "But now apart from law a righteousness of God is revealed," he means "any law"; and the expression could be translated "apart from law-method." This difference is clearly seen in the use of ὁ Θεός and Θεός. ὁ Θεός is used of the divine Person "God." Θεός is used (generally) of the divine character or essence of God. Thus "in the

129

beginning was the Word and the Word was with God (τὸν Θεόν) and the Word was divine (Θεός)" gives the sense. In a similar way in Romans 1-3 such terms as ὀργὴ Θεοῦ and δικαιοσύνη Θεοῦ may well be translated "divine wrath" and "divine righteousness." An extensive discussion of this usage is found in Dana and Mantey, *A Manual Grammar of the Greek New Testament*.

(1) Ordinary use of the Greek article:

1. To point out particular objects, ὁ ἄνθρωπος, ἡ βασιλεία, etc.
2. With abstract nouns where English usage omits the article, ἡ ἀλήθεια, ἡ χάρις, ἡ ἐλπίς.
3. With proper nouns where English usage omits the article, ὁ Πέτρος, ὁ Ἰησοῦς.
4. With classes or groups where English usage omits the article αἱ ἀλώπεκες, τὰ πετεινά, "foxes, birds."
5. With pronouns. This usage with αὐτός, οὗτος, ἐκεῖνος, and πᾶς has been observed in previous study.
6. With adverbs. ἀπὸ τοῦ νῦν, "from the now" really means "from the present time."
7. With infinitives. ἐν τῷ σπείρειν, "in the to sow" really means "while he was sowing." This usage will be noted at length in the next lesson. In such a construction the article is always neuter.
8. With prepositional phrases. οἱ ἐν τῷ οἴκῳ means "the in the house ones" or "the men who are in the house."

(2) Special use of the Greek article:

1. With the conjunction καί.

When two nouns are joined by the conjunction καί:

a. If both nouns have the definite article they refer to different persons (or things). ὁ ἀπόστολος καὶ ὁ μαθητής . . . These are two people.
b. If the first of the two nouns has the article and the second does not, the two are one person (or thing). ὁ ἀπόστολος καὶ μαθητής. This is one person.

130

2. With the conjunction μέν . . . δέ:

The use of the article with μέν and δέ gives the force of an alternative pronoun. οἱ μὲν ἦσαν σὺν τοῖς Ἰουδαίοις, οἱ δὲ σὺν τοῖς ἀποστόλοις. "*Some* were with the Jews, but *others* were with the apostles" (Acts 14:4).

3. With the force of a demonstrative pronoun:

οἱ οὖν ἠρώτων αὐτόν. "*These*, therefore, were asking him."

4. With the force of a possessive pronoun:

συνεπέμψαμεν μετ᾽ αὐτοῦ τὸν ἀδελφόν. "We have sent with him *his* brother."

5. With the force of a relative pronoun:

τοῦτο γάρ ἐστιν τὸ αἷμα μου τῆς διαθήκης τὸ περὶ πολλῶν ἐκχυννόμενον. "For this is my blood of the new covenant *which* is shed for many."

6. With nouns joined by forms of εἰμί.

When two substantives are joined by the verb εἰμί:
a. If one only has the definite article, it is to be regarded as the subject of the sentence and the anarthrous one as the predicate. ὁ Θεὸς ἀγάπη ἐστίν.
b. If both substantives have the article, they are inter- changeable as to subject and predicate. ἡ δύναμις τῆς ἁμαρτίας ἐστὶν ὁ νόμος. "The power of sin is the law" or "The law is the power of sin."

The above analysis does not attempt an exhaustive treatment of the function of the Greek article. It is to serve as a guide to introduce to the beginner the wide and significant usage of this construction in the Greek New Testament.

101. Practical Application

Translate 1 John 2:12-17.

LESSON 33

THE INFINITIVE

102. Lexical Study

ἀντίχριστος, ὁ, antichrist
ἀρνέομαι, I deny
ἐπαγγέλλω, I announce
οἶδα, I know (perfect tense
of obsolete εἴδω; always
used with force of pres-
ent tense)

ὁμολογέω, I confess
φανερόω, I make manifest
χρῖσμα, -ατος, τό,
anointing
ψεῦδος, -ους, τό, lie

103. Grammatical Study

It has been observed in previous study that the infinitive is a verbal noun and that it is not inflected. Observe the forms in the paradigm in the back of the book. The following analysis will guide the beginner into the extensive use of the Greek infinitive. This does not include the very obvious usage of the infinitive after verbs of wishing, etc.

(1) The Infinitive as a Verb

Character: As a verb the infinitive has voice and tense.

Usage: As a verb the infinitive may take an object and it may be modified by adverbs. The following are the most frequently found verbal uses:

1. To express the purpose of the main verb.

μὴ νομίσητε ὅτι ἦλθον καταλῦσαι τὸν νόμον. "Do not conclude that I have come to destroy the law."

2. To express the result of the main verb. There is the possibility of confusion at this point between "purpose" and "result." Some instances are clearly "result" clauses; others are subject to interpretation. For the fine points of "intended result," "actual result," and "conceived result" see Dana and Mantey *in loco*. ἐγένετο ὡσεὶ νεκρός, ὥστε τοὺς πολλοὺς λέγειν ὅτι ἀπέθανεν. "He became as a dead man so that many said that he had died." The noun or pronoun indicating the persons involved in producing the action of an infinitive is always in the accusative case. This is called by some "the subject of the infinitive in the accusative case" and by others an "accusative of general reference describing the persons involved in the action."

3. To express temporal ideas:

   a. "Before" is expressed by the infinitive and πρίν or πρὶν ἤ. Example: Κύριε, κατάβηθι πρὶν ἀποθανεῖν τὸ παιδίον μου. "Lord, come down before my child dies." This idea can also be expressed by πρὸ τοῦ and the infinitive.

   b. "While" is expressed by the infinitive and ἐν τῷ. ἐθαύμαζον ἐν τῷ χρονίζειν ἐν τῷ ναῷ αὐτόν. "They were wondering while he was tarrying in the temple."

   c. "After" is expressed by the infinitive and μετὰ τό. παρέστησεν ἑαυτὸν ζῶντα μετὰ τὸ παθεῖν αὐτόν. "He showed himself alive after his suffering."

4. To express cause the infinitive is used with διὰ τό. οὐκ ἔχετε διὰ τὸ μὴ αἰτεῖσθαι ὑμᾶς. "You have not because you ask not."

(2) The Infinitive as a Noun

Character: Originally it was inflected as a noun, but the inflection has been lost.

Usage: The infinitive may be used in any way a noun can be used.

1. As the subject of a finite verb.

οὐχ ὑμῶν ἐστιν γνῶναι χρόνους ἢ καιρούς. "To know times and seasons . . . is not yours."

133

2. As the direct object of a verb.

ὁ Ἰησοῦς ἤρξατο ποιεῖν καὶ διδάσκειν. "Jesus began to do and to teach."

3. As the secondary object of a verb.

ἔχω σοί τι εἰπεῖν. "I have something [direct object] to say [secondary object] to you."

4. As an appositional substantive.

θρησκεία καθαρὰ . . . αὕτη ἐστίν, ἐπισκέπτεσθαι ὀρφανοὺς . . . "Pure religion . . . is this, to visit orphans . . ."

5. As a modifier. Illustrations of the infinitive used as a substantive modifier abound in the New Testament. ἦλθεν ὁ καιρὸς τῶν νεκρῶν κριθῆναι. "The time of the dead to be judged has come." Here the infinitive modifies a noun. It may also modify an adjective. φρουρουμένους διὰ πίστεως εἰς σωτηρίαν ἑτοίμην ἀποκαλυφθῆναι . . . "kept through faith unto salvation ready to be revealed."

104. Practical Application

Translate 1 John 2:18-29.

134

PARADIGMS

NOUNS

105. First Declension Feminine

Singular

	kingdom	day	tongue	writing
N. V.	βασιλεία	ἡμέρα	γλῶσσα	γραφή
G. A.	βασιλείας	ἡμέρας	γλώσσης	γραφῆς
D. L. I.	βασιλείᾳ	ἡμέρᾳ	γλώσσῃ	γραφῇ
A.	βασιλείαν	ἡμέραν	γλῶσσαν	γραφήν

Plural

N. V.	βασιλεῖαι	ἡμέραι	γλῶσσαι	γραφαί
G. A.	βασιλειῶν	ἡμερῶν	γλωσσῶν	γραφῶν
D. L. I.	βασιλείαις	ἡμέραις	γλώσσαις	γραφαῖς
A.	βασιλείας	ἡμέρας	γλώσσας	γραφάς

First Declension Masculine

Singular

	Messiah	prophet
N.	Μεσσίας	προφήτης
G. A.	Μεσσίου	προφήτου
D. L. I.	Μεσσίᾳ	προφήτῃ
A.	Μεσσίαν	προφήτην
V.	Μεσσία	προφῆτα

Plural

N. V.	Μεσσίαι	προφῆται
G. A.	Μεσσιῶν	προφητῶν
D. L. I.	Μεσσίαις	προφήταις
A.	Μεσσίας	προφήτας

135

106. Second Declension Masculine and Feminine

Singular

	word	servant	man	way
N.	λόγος, ὁ	δοῦλος, ὁ	ἄνθρωπος, ὁ	ὁδός, ἡ
G. A.	λόγου	δούλου	ἀνθρώπου	ὁδοῦ
D. L. I.	λόγῳ	δούλῳ	ἀνθρώπῳ	ὁδῷ
A.	λόγον	δοῦλον	ἄνθρωπον	ὁδόν
V.	λόγε	δοῦλε	ἄνθρωπε	ὁδέ

Plural

N. V.	λόγοι	δοῦλοι	ἄνθρωποι	ὁδοί
G. A.	λόγων	δούλων	ἀνθρώπων	ὁδῶν
D. L. I.	λόγοις	δούλοις	ἀνθρώποις	ὁδοῖς
A.	λόγους	δούλους	ἀνθρώπους	ὁδούς

Second Declension Neuter

Singular

	gift	temple
N. V.	δῶρον	ἱερόν
G. A.	δώρου	ἱεροῦ
D. L. I.	δώρῳ	ἱερῷ
A.	δῶρον	ἱερόν

Plural

N. V.	δῶρα	ἱερά
G. A.	δώρων	ἱερῶν
D. L. I.	δώροις	ἱεροῖς
A.	δῶρα	ἱερά

107. Third Declension

Liquid	Mute	Syncopated

Singular

	age	hope	grace	night	father
N.	αἰών, ὁ	ἐλπίς, ἡ	χάρις, ἡ	νύξ, ἡ	πατήρ, ὁ
G. A.	αἰῶνος	ἐλπίδος	χάριτος	νυκτός	πατρός
D. L. I.	αἰῶνι	ἐλπίδι	χάριτι	νυκτί	πατρί
A.	αἰῶνα	ἐλπίδα	χάριν	νύκτα	πατέρα
V.	αἰών	ἐλπί	χάρις	νύξ	πάτερ

Plural

	age	hope	grace	night	father
N. V.	αἰῶνες	ἐλπίδες	χάριτες	νύκτες	πατέρες
G. A.	αἰώνων	ἐλπίδων	χαρίτων	νυκτῶν	πατέρων
D. L. I.	αἰῶσι	ἐλπίσι(ν)	χάρισι(ν)	νυξί(ν)	πατράσι(ν)
A.	αἰῶνας	ἐλπίδας	χάριτας	νύκτας	πατέρας

Vowel Stems

Singular

	faith	king	fish
N.	πίστις, ἡ	βασιλεύς, ο	ἰχθύς, ὁ
G. A.	πίστεως	βασιλέως	ἰχθύος
D. L. I.	πίστει	βασιλεῖ	ἰχθύι
A.	πίστιν	βασιλέα	ἰχθύν
V.	πίστι	βασιλεῦ	ἰχθύ

Plural

	faith	king	fish
N. V.	πίστεις	βασιλεῖς	ἰχθύες
G. A.	πίστεων	βασιλέων	ἰχθύων
D. L. I.	πίστεσι(ν)	βασιλεῦσι(ν)	ἰχθύσι
A.	πίστεις	βασιλεῖς	ἰχθύας (ἰχθῦς)

Neuter

Singular

	race	body
N. V.	γένος	σῶμα
G. A.	γένους	σώματος
D. L. I.	γένει	σώματι
A.	γένος	σῶμα

Plural

N. V.	γένη	σώματα
G. A.	γενῶν	σωμάτων
D. L. I.	γένεσι (ν)	σώμασι
A.	γένη	σώματα

THE ARTICLE

108. ὁ, ἡ, τό, the

	Singular			Plural		
	M.	F.	N.	M.	F.	N.
N.	ὁ	ἡ	τό	οἱ	αἱ	τά
G. A.	τοῦ	τῆς	τοῦ	τῶν	τῶν	τῶν
D. L. I.	τῷ	τῇ	τῷ	τοῖς	ταῖς	τοῖς
A.	τόν	τήν	τό	τούς	τάς	τά

ADJECTIVES

109. Second and First Declension Analogy

Singular　　　　　　Plural

good

	M.	F.	N.	M.	F.	N.
N.	ἀγαθός	ἀγαθή	ἀγαθόν	ἀγαθοί	ἀγαθαί	ἀγαθά
G. A.	ἀγαθοῦ	ἀγαθῆς	ἀγαθοῦ	ἀγαθῶν	ἀγαθῶν	ἀγαθῶν
D. L. I.	ἀγαθῷ	ἀγαθῇ	ἀγαθῷ	ἀγαθοῖς	ἀγαθαῖς	ἀγαθοῖς
A.	ἀγαθόν	ἀγαθήν	ἀγαθόν	ἀγαθούς	ἀγαθάς	ἀγαθά
V.	ἀγαθέ	ἀγαθή	ἀγαθόν	ἀγαθοί	ἀγαθαί	ἀγαθά

Singular　　　　　　Plural

small

	M.	F.	N.	M.	F.	N.
N.	μικρός	μικρά	μικρόν	μικροί	μικραί	μικρά
G. A.	μικροῦ	μικρᾶς	μικροῦ	μικρῶν	μικρῶν	μικρῶν
D. L. I.	μικρῷ	μικρᾷ	μικρῷ	μικροῖς	μικραῖς	μικροῖς
A.	μικρόν	μικράν	μικρόν	μικρούς	μικράς	μικρά
V.	μικρέ	μικρά	μικρόν	μικροί	μικραί	μικρά

Singular   Plural

righteous

	M.	F.	N.	M.	F.	N.
N.	δίκαιος	δικαία	δίκαιον	δίκαιοι	δίκαιαι	δίκαια
G. A.	δικαίου	δικαίας	δικαίου	δικαίων	δικαίων	δικαίων
D. L. I.	δικαίῳ	δικαίᾳ	δικαίῳ	δικαίοις	δικαίαις	δικαίοις
A.	δίκαιον	δικαίαν	δίκαιον	δικαίους	δικαίας	δίκαια
V.	δίκαιε	δικαία	δίκαιον	δίκαιοι	δίκαιαι	δίκαια

Irregular

Singular   Plural

great

	M.	F.	N.	M.	F.	N.
N.	μέγας	μεγάλη	μέγα	μεγάλοι	μεγάλαι	μεγάλα
G. A.	μεγάλου	μεγάλης	μεγάλου	μεγάλων	μεγάλων	μεγάλων
D. L. I.	μεγάλῳ	μεγάλη	μεγάλῳ	μεγάλοις	μεγάλαις	μεγάλοις
A.	μέγαν	μεγάλην	μέγα	μεγάλους	μεγάλας	μεγάλα
V.	μεγάλε	μεγάλη	μέγα	μεγάλοι	μεγάλαι	μεγάλα

Singular   Plural

much

	M.	F.	N.	M.	F.	N.
N.	πολύς	πολλή	πολύ	πολλοί	πολλαί	πολλά
G. A.	πολλοῦ	πολλῆς	πολλοῦ	πολλῶν	πολλῶν	πολλῶν
D. L. I.	πολλῷ	πολλῇ	πολλῷ	πολλοῖς	πολλαῖς	πολλοῖς
A.	πολύν	πολλήν	πολύ	πολλούς	πολλάς	πολλά

110. Third and First Declension Analogy

Singular   Plural

all

	M.	F.	N.	M.	F.	N.
N.	πᾶς	πᾶσα	πᾶν	πάντες	πᾶσαι	πάντα
G. A.	παντός	πάσης	παντός	πάντων	πασῶν	πάντων
D. L. I.	παντί	πάσῃ	παντί	πᾶσι(ν)	πάσαις	πᾶσι(ν)
A.	πάντα	πᾶσαν	πᾶν	πάντας	πάσας	πάντα

139

111. Third Declension Analogy

	Singular		Plural	
			true	
	M. and F.	N.	M. and F.	N.
N.	ἀληθής	ἀληθές	ἀληθεῖς	ἀληθῆ
G. A.	ἀληθοῦς	ἀληθοῦς	ἀληθῶν	ἀληθῶν
D. L. I.	ἀληθεῖ	ἀληθεῖ	ἀληθέσι (ν)	ἀληθέσι (ν)
A.	ἀληθῆ	ἀληθές	ἀληθεῖς	ἀληθῆ
V.	ἀληθές	ἀληθές	ἀληθεῖς	ἀληθῆ

	Singular		Plural	
			greater	
	M. and F.	N.	M. and F.	N.
N.	μείζων	μεῖζον	μείζονες (μείζους)	μείζονα (μείζω)
G. A.	μείζονος	μείζονος	μειζόνων	μειζόνων
D. L. I.	μείζονι	μείζονι	μείζοσι (ν)	μείζοσι (ν)
A.	μείζονα (μείζω)	μεῖζον	μείζονας (μείζους)	μείζονα (μείζω)

PRONOUNS

112. Personal

Singular

	First, I	Second, you	Third, he, she, it		
N.	ἐγώ	σύ	αὐτός	αὐτή	αὐτό
G. A.	ἐμοῦ (μου)	σοῦ (σου)	αὐτοῦ	αὐτῆς	αὐτοῦ
D. L. I.	ἐμοί (μοι)	σοί (σοι)	αὐτῷ	αὐτῇ	αὐτῷ
A.	ἐμέ (με)	σέ (σε)	αὐτόν	αὐτήν	αὐτό

Plural

N.	ἡμεῖς	ὑμεῖς	αὐτοί	αὐταί	αὐτά
G. A.	ἡμῶν	ὑμῶν	αὐτῶν	αὐτῶν	αὐτῶν
D. L. I.	ἡμῖν	ὑμῖν	αὐτοῖς	αὐταῖς	αὐτοῖς
A.	ἡμᾶς	ὑμᾶς	αὐτούς	αὐτάς	αὐτά

113. Demonstrative

	Singular				Plural		
			this				
	M.	F.	N.		M.	F.	N.
N.	οὗτος	αὕτη	τοῦτο		οὗτοι	αὗται	ταῦτα
G. A.	τούτου	ταύτης	τούτου		τούτων	τούτων	τούτων
D. L. I.	τούτῳ	ταύτῃ	τούτῳ		τούτοις	ταύταις	τούτοις
A.	τοῦτον	ταύτην	τοῦτο		τούτους	ταύτας	ταῦτα

	Singular				Plural		
			that				
	M.	F.	N.		M.	F.	N.
N.	ἐκεῖνος	ἐκείνη	ἐκεῖνο		ἐκεῖνοι	ἐκεῖναι	ἐκεῖνα
G. A.	ἐκείνου	ἐκείνης	ἐκείνου		ἐκείνων	ἐκείνων	ἐκείνων
D. L. I.	ἐκείνῳ	ἐκείνῃ	ἐκείνῳ		ἐκείνοις	ἐκείναις	ἐκείνοις
A.	ἐκεῖνον	ἐκείνην	ἐκεῖνο		ἐκείνους	ἐκείνας	ἐκεῖνα

114. Relative, who, which

	Singular			Plural		
	M.	F.	N.	M.	F.	N.
N.	ὅς	ἥ	ὅ	οἵ	αἵ	ἅ
G. A.	οὗ	ἧς	οὗ	ὧν	ὧν	ὧν
D. L. I.	ᾧ	ᾗ	ᾧ	οἷς	αἷς	οἷς
A.	ὅν	ἥν	ὅ	οὕς	ἅς	ἅ

115. Interrogative, who?, which?

	Singular		Plural	
	M. and F.	N.	M. and F.	N.
N.	τίς	τί	τίνες	τίνα
G. A.	τίνος	τίνος	τίνων	τίνων
D. L. I.	τίνι	τίνι	τίσι	τίσι
A.	τίνα	τί	τίνας	τίνα

116. The indefinite pronoun is declined like τίς, τί but the forms are enclitic.

117. The indefinite relative (or qualitative relative) is found only in the nominative forms in the New Testament; translated who or whoever.

	Singular			Plural		
	M.	F.	N.	M.	F.	N.
	ὅστις	ἥτις	ὅτι	οἵτινες	αἵτινες	ἅτινα

118. Reflexive

<table>
<tr><th colspan="3">First Person, myself</th><th colspan="2">Second Person, yourself</th></tr>
<tr><th></th><th>M.</th><th>F.</th><th>M.</th><th>F.</th></tr>
<tr><td>G. A.</td><td>ἐμαυτοῦ</td><td>ἐμαυτῆς</td><td>σεαυτοῦ</td><td>σεαυτῆς</td></tr>
<tr><td>D. L. I.</td><td>ἐμαυτῷ</td><td>ἐμαυτῇ</td><td>σεαυτῷ</td><td>σεαυτῇ</td></tr>
<tr><td>A.</td><td>ἐμαυτόν</td><td>ἐμαυτήν</td><td>σεαυτόν</td><td>σεαυτήν</td></tr>
</table>

Plural

<table>
<tr><th></th><th>M.</th><th>F.</th><th>M.</th><th>F.</th></tr>
<tr><td>G. A.</td><td>ἑαυτῶν</td><td>ἑαυτῶν</td><td>ἑαυτῶν</td><td>ἑαυτῶν</td></tr>
<tr><td>D. L. I.</td><td>ἑαυτοῖς</td><td>ἑαυταῖς</td><td>ἑαυτοῖς</td><td>ἑαυταῖς</td></tr>
<tr><td>A.</td><td>ἑαυτούς</td><td>ἑαυτάς</td><td>ἑαυτούς</td><td>ἑαυτάς</td></tr>
</table>

Third Person, himself, herself, itself

<table>
<tr><th colspan="4">Singular</th><th colspan="3">Plural</th></tr>
<tr><th></th><th>M.</th><th>F.</th><th>N.</th><th>M.</th><th>F.</th><th>N.</th></tr>
<tr><td>G. A.</td><td>ἑαυτοῦ</td><td>ἑαυτῆς</td><td>ἑαυτοῦ</td><td>ἑαυτῶν</td><td>ἑαυτῶν</td><td>ἑαυτῶν</td></tr>
<tr><td>D. L. I.</td><td>ἑαυτῷ</td><td>ἑαυτῇ</td><td>ἑαυτῷ</td><td>ἑαυτοῖς</td><td>ἑαυταῖς</td><td>ἑαυτοῖς</td></tr>
<tr><td>A.</td><td>ἑαυτόν</td><td>ἑαυτήν</td><td>ἑαυτό</td><td>ἑαυτούς</td><td>ἑαυτάς</td><td>ἑαυτά</td></tr>
</table>

119. Reciprocal, of each other, three forms only in the Greek New Testament:

G. A.	ἀλλήλων
D. L. I.	ἀλλήλοις
A.	ἀλλήλους

142

120. Possessive

First Person, my

Singular

	M.	F.	N.	M.	F.	N.
N.	ἐμός	ἐμή	ἐμόν	ἐμοί	ἐμαί	ἐμά
G. A.	ἐμοῦ	ἐμῆς	ἐμοῦ	ἐμῶν	ἐμῶν	ἐμῶν
D. L. I.	ἐμῷ	ἐμῇ	ἐμῷ	ἐμοῖς	ἐμαῖς	ἐμοῖς
A.	ἐμόν	ἐμήν	ἐμόν	ἐμούς	ἐμάς	ἐμά

Second Person, your
Declined like ἐμός, etc.: σός, σή, σόν

Third Person, his, hers, its
Declined like ἐμός, etc.: ἴδιος, ἰδία, ἴδιον

First Person plural, our
Declined like ἐμός, etc.: ἡμέτερος, α, ον

Second Person plural, your
Declined like ἐμός, etc.: ὑμέτερος, α, ον

121. Alternative, other, ἄλλος, ἄλλη, ἄλλο — regular in declension.

122. Negative, no one

	With indicative mood			With other moods		
	M.	F.	N.	M.	F.	N.
N.	οὐδείς	οὐδεμία	οὐδέν	μηδείς	μηδεμία	μηδέν
G. A.	οὐδενός	οὐδεμᾶς	οὐδενός	μηδενός	μηδεμᾶς	μηδενός
D. L. I.	οὐδενί	οὐδεμιᾷ	οὐδενί	μηδενί	μηδεμιᾷ	μηδενί
A.	οὐδένα	οὐδεμίαν	οὐδέν	μηδένα	μηδεμίαν	μηδέν

143

VERBS

123. εἰμί, I am

Indicative Mood

Present		Imperfect		Future	
S.	P.	S.	P.	S.	P.
εἰμί	ἐσμέν	ἤμην	ἦμεν	ἔσομαι	ἐσόμεθα
εἶ	ἐστέ	ἦς	ἦτε	ἔσῃ	ἔσεσθε
ἐστί	εἰσί	ἦν	ἦσαν	ἔσται	ἔσονται

Subjunctive Mood

S.	P.
ὦ	ὦμεν
ᾖς	ἦτε
ᾖ	ὦσι

Imperative Mood

S.	P.
—	—
ἴσθι	ἔστε
ἔστω	ἔστωσαν

Infinitive

εἶναι

Participle

	Singular			Plural		
	M.	F.	N.	M.	F.	N.
N.	ὤν	οὖσα	ὄν	ὄντες	οὖσαι	ὄντα
G. A.	ὄντος	οὔσης	ὄντος	ὄντων	οὐσῶν	ὄντων
D. L. I.	ὄντι	οὔσῃ	ὄντι	οὖσι(ν)	οὔσαις	οὖσι(ν)
A.	ὄντα	οὖσαν	ὄν	ὄντας	οὔσας	ὄντα

144

VOCABULARY

ENGLISH — GREEK

Abide,
  μένω
About,
  περί
After,
  μετά
Age,
  αἰών
All,
  πᾶς
Already,
  ἤδη
Also,
  καί
Am,
  εἰμί
And,
  καί
Angel,
  ἄγγελος
Announce,
  ἀναγγέλλω, ἐπαγγέλομαι
Anointing,
  χρίσμα
Answer,
  ἀποκρίνομαι
Antichrist,
  ἀντίχριστος
Apostle,
  ἀπόστολος
Around,
  περί
As,
  ὡς
Ashamed,
  αἰσχύνομαι

Bad,
  κακός

Baptize,
  βαπτίζω
Bear,
  φέρω
Because,
  ὅτι
Become,
  γίνομαι
Before,
  πρίν, πρό
Beget,
  γεννάω
Begin,
  ἄρχομαι
Beginning,
  ἀρχή
Behold,
  θεωρέω
Believe,
  πιστεύω
Beloved,
  ἀγαπητός
Bless,
  εὐλογέω
Blessed,
  μακάριος
Blind,
  τυφλόω
Blind man,
  τυφλός
Blood,
  αἷμα
Boat,
  πλοῖον
Body,
  σῶμα
Boldness,
  παρρησία
Book,
  βιβλίον

145

Bread,
   ἄρτος
Bring,
   φέρω
Brother,
   ἀδελφός
But,
   ἀλλά, δέ, μέν . . . δέ
But not,
   οὐδέ, μηδέ
By,
   ὑπό, διά, παρά

Call,
   καλέω
Cast,
   βάλλω
Chief-priest,
   ἀρχιερεύς
Child,
   τέκνον
Christ,
   Χριστός
Church,
   ἐκκλησία
City,
   πόλις
Cleanse,
   καθαρίζω
Come,
   ἔρχομαι
Come near,
   ἐγγίζω
Comfort,
   παρακαλέω
Comforter,
   παράκλητος
Coming,
   παρουσία
Commandment,
   ἐντολή
Confess,
   ὁμολογέω

Conquer,
   νικάω
Corn,
   στάχυς
Crowd,
   ὄχλος
Crucify,
   σταυρόω
Custom,
   ἔθος

Darkness,
   σκότος, σκοτία
Daughter,
   θυγάτηρ
Day,
   ἡμέρα
Dead,
   νεκρός
Death,
   θάνατος
Deceive,
   πλανάω, ψεύδομαι
Demon,
   δαιμόνιον
Deny,
   ἀρνέομαι
Depth,
   βάθος
Desert,
   ἔρημος
Desire,
   ἐπιθυμία
Destroy,
   λύω
Detest,
   μισέω
Die,
   ἀποθνήσκω
Disciple,
   μαθητής
Do,
   ποιέω

Down,
κατά
Draw near,
ἐγγίζω
Drink,
πίνω

Ear,
οὖς
Eat,
ἐσθίω
Empty talk,
ἀλαζονία
End,
τέλος
Even,
καί
Even as,
καθώς
Every,
πᾶς
Evil,
πονηρός
Eye,
ὀφθαλμός

Faith,
πίστις
Faithful,
πιστός
Fall,
πίπτω
Father,
πατήρ
Fellowship,
κοινωνία
First,
πρῶτος
Fish,
ἰχθύς
Fisherman,
ἀλιεύς

Flesh,
σάρξ
For,
γάρ
Forgive,
ἀφίημι
From,
ἀπό, ἐκ, παρά
Fruit,
καρπός

Gather together,
συνάγω
Gentiles,
ἔθνη
Genuine,
ἀληθινός
Gift,
δῶρον
Give,
δίδωμι
Give thanks,
εὐχαριστέω
Glorify,
δοξάζω
Go,
βαίνω, ἔρχομαι, πορεύομαι
Go away,
ὑπάγω
God,
Θεός
Good,
ἀγαθός, καλός
Gospel,
εὐαγγέλιον
Grace,
χάρις
Great,
μέγας

Hand,
χείρ

147

Hate,
   μισέω
Have,
   ἔχω
He,
   αὐτός
Heal,
   θεραπεύω
Hear,
   ἀκούω
Heart,
   καρδία
Heaven,
   οὐρανός
Herself,
   ἑαυτῆς
Himself,
   ἑαυτοῦ
His
   ἴδιος
Holy,
   ἅγιος
Honor,
   τιμάω
Hope,
   ἐλπίς
Hour,
   ὥρα
House,
   οἰκία, οἶκος

I,
   ἐγώ
If,
   εἰ, ἐάν
In,
   ἐν
In order that,
   ἵνα
Instead of,
   ἀντί, ὑπέρ
Into,
   εἰς

It,
   αὐτό
Itself,
   ἑαυτοῦ

Jesus,
   Ἰησοῦς
Joy,
   χαρά
Judge,
   κρίνω
Judgment,
   κρίσις
Just,
   δίκαιος,
Just as,
   καθώς

Keep,
   τηρέω
Kill,
   ἀποκτείνω
King,
   βασιλεύς
Kingdom,
   βασιλεία
Kingly,
   βασιλικός
Know,
   γινώσκω, οἶδα
Knowledge,
   γνῶσις

Language,
   γλῶσσα
Last,
   ἔσχατος
Law,
   νόμος
Lead,
   ἄγω

148

Lead astray,
πλανάω
Leave,
λείπω
Liar,
ψεύστης
Lie,
ψεύδομαι
Lie,
ψεῦδος
Life,
βίος, ψυχή, ζωή
Light,
φῶς
Like,
ὡς
Little,
μικρός
Loose,
λύω
Lord,
κύριος
Love,
ἀγαπάω, φιλέω
Love,
ἀγάπη
Lust,
ἐπιθυμία

Make,
ποιέω
Make manifest,
δηλόω, φανερόω
Man,
ἄνθρωπος
Marriage,
γάμος
Mercy,
ἔλεος
Message,
ἀγγελία
Messenger,
ἄγγελος

Messiah,
Μεσσίας
Mother,
μήτηρ
Mountain,
ὄρος
Mouth,
στόμα
Much,
πολύς
Multitude,
ὄχλος
My,
ἐμός
Myself,
ἐμαυτοῦ

Name,
ὄνομα
Nation,
ἔθνος
Need,
χρεία
Neither . . . nor,
οὐδέ . . . οὐδέ, μηδέ . . . μηδέ
New,
καινός
Night,
νύξ
No longer,
οὐκέτι, μηκέτι
No one,
οὐδείς, μηδείς
Nor,
οὐδέ, μηδέ
Not,
οὐ, μή
Not yet,
μηκέτι, οὔπω
Now,
ἄρτι, νῦν

Offense,
σκάνδαλον

149

Old,
   παλαιός
On,
   ἐπί
On account of,
   διά
Only,
   μόνος
Other,
   ἄλλος, ἕτερος
Ought,
   ὀφείλω
Our,
   ἡμέτερος
Overcome,
   νικάω
Owe,
   ὀφείλω

Parable,
   παραβολή
Peace,
   εἰρήνη
People,
   λαός
Perfect,
   τελειόω
Place,
   τίθημι
Place,
   τόπος
Power,
   δύναμις
Praise,
   δόξα
Pray,
   προσεύχομαι
Preach,
   κηρύσσω, εὐαγγελίζομαι
Prepare,
   ἑτοιμάζω
Presence,
   παρουσία

Priest,
   ἱερεύς
Profess,
   ὁμολογέω
Promise,
   ἐπαγγελία
Prophet,
   προφήτης
Propitiation,
   ἱλασμός
Purify,
   καθαρίζω
Put,
   τίθημι

Race,
   γένος
Raise up,
   ἐγείρω
Read,
   ἀναγινώσκω
Receive,
   δέχομαι, λαμβάνω
Remain,
   μένω
Remaining,
   λοιποί
Resurrection,
   ἀνάστασις
Righteous,
   δίκαιος
Righteousness,
   δικαιοσύνη
Road,
   ὁδός
Royal,
   βασιλικός
Rule,
   ἄρχω
Ruler,
   ἄρχων

Saints,
   οἱ ἅγιοι

150

Salvation,	Sow,
σωτηρία	σπείρω
Sanctify	Speak,
ἁγιάζω	λαλέω
Save,	Spirit,
σώζω	πνεῦμα
Say,	Stand,
λέγω	ἵστημι
Scribe,	Still,
γραμματεύς	ἔτι
Scripture,	Stone,
γραφή	λίθος
Sea,	Strife,
θάλασσα	στάσις
See,	Strong,
βλέπω, ὁράω	ἰσχυρός
Seek,	Stumbling-block,
ζητέω	σκάνδαλον
Send,	Suffer,
πέμπω, ἀποστέλλω	πάσχω
Servant,	Sufficient,
δοῦλος	ἰσχυρός
She,	Synagogue,
αὐτή	συναγωγή
Shine,	
φαίνω	
Show,	Take,
δηλόω	λαμβάνω
Sin,	Take up,
ἁμαρτάνω	αἴρω
Sin,	Teach,
ἁμαρτία	διδάσκω
Sinner,	Teacher,
ἁμαρτωλός	διδάσκαλος
Slave,	Teaching,
δοῦλος	διδαχή
Small,	Temple,
μικρός	ἱερόν
So,	Testimony,
οὕτως	μαρτυρία
Someone,	That,
τις	ὅτι, ἵνα
Son,	That,
υἱός	ἐκεῖνος

The,
ὁ, ἡ, τό
Then,
τότε
This,
οὗτος
Through,
διά
Thus,
οὕτως
To,
πρός
Tongue,
γλῶσσα
Toward,
πρός
True,
ἀληθινός, ἀληθής
Truly,
ἀληθῶς
Truth,
ἀλήθεια

Unrighteous,
ἀδικία
Until,
ἄχρι, ἕως
Up,
ἀνά

Vainglory,
ἀλαζονία
Voice,
φωνή

Walk,
περιπατέω

Water,
ὕδωρ
Way,
ὁδός
Whence,
ὅθεν
Which,
ὅς, τίς
Who,
ὅς, ὅστις, τίς
Whole,
ὅλος, πᾶς
Will,
θέλημα
Wish,
θέλω
With,
μετά, σύν
Witness,
μαρτυρία
Wonder,
θαυμάζω
Word,
λόγος, ῥῆμα
Work,
ἔργον
World,
κόσμος
Write,
γράφω

You,
σύ
Young man,
νεανίσκος
Your,
σός, ὑμέτερος
Yourself,
σεαυτοῦ

ἀγαθός, ή, όν,
 good
ἀγαπάω, ἀγαπήσω, ἠγάπησα, ἠγάπηκα, ἠγάπημαι, ἠγαπήθην,
 I love
ἀγάπη, ἡ,
 love
ἀγαπητός, ή, όν,
 beloved
ἀγγελία, ἡ,
 message
ἄγγελος, ὁ,
 messenger, angel
ἀγιάζω, ——, ἡγίησα, ——, ἡγίασμαι, ἡγιάσθην,
 I sanctify
ἅγιος, α, ον,
 holy (οἱ ἅγιοι, the saints)
ἄγω, ἄξω, ἤγαγον, ——, ἤχθην,
 I lead
ἀδελφός, ὁ,
 brother
ἀδικία, ἡ,
 unrighteousness
αἷμα, αἵματος, τό,
 blood
αἴρω, ἀρῶ, ἦρα, ἦρκα, ἦρμαι, ἤρθην,
 I take up (or away)
αἰών, αἰῶνος, ὁ,
 age
αἰσχύνομαι, (aor. pass., ἠσχύνθην),
 I am ashamed
ἀκούω, ἀκούσω, ἤκουσα, ἀκήκοα, ——, ἠκούσθην,
 I hear
ἀλαζονία, ἡ,
 empty talk, vainglory
ἀλήθεια, ἡ,
 truth
ἀληθινός, ή, όν,
 genuine, true
ἀληθής, ές,
 true, unhidden
ἀληθῶς,
 adv., truly

153

ἁλιεύς, ἁλιέως, ὁ,
    fisherman
ἀλλά,
    conj., but
ἄλλος, η, ο,
    other (usually another of the same kind)
ἁμαρτάνω, ἁμαρτήσω, ἡμάρτησα (or ἥμαρτον), ἡμάρτηκα, _____, _____,
    I sin
ἁμαρτία, ἡ,
    sin
ἁμαρτωλός, ὁ,
    sinner
ἄν,
    cond. or temp. particle usually not translated
ἀνά,
    prep. with acc., up, again
ἀναβαίνω,
    I go up (see βαίνω for principal parts)
ἀναγγέλλω, ἀναγγελῶ, ἀνήγγειλα, _____, _____, ἀνηγγέλην,
    I announce
ἀναγινώσκω,
    I read (see γινώσκω for principal parts)
ἀνάστασις, ἀναστάσεως, ἡ,
    resurrection
ἄνθρωπος, ὁ,
    man
ἀντί,
    prep. with gen., against, instead of
ἀντίχριστος, ὁ,
    antichrist
ἀπό,
    prep. with abl., away from
ἀποθνήσκω, ἀποθανοῦμαι, ἀπέθανον, _____, _____, _____,
    I die
ἀποκρίνομαι, ἀποκρινοῦμαι, ἀπεκρινάμην, _____, _____, ἀπεκρίθην,
    I answer
ἀποκτείνω, ἀποκτενῶ, ἀπέκτεινα, _____, _____, ἀπεκτάνθην,
    I kill
ἀποστέλλω, ἀποστελῶ, ἀπέστειλα, ἀπέσταλκα, ἀπέσταλμαι, ἀπεστάλην,
    I send (with a message)
ἀπόστολος, ὁ,
    an apostle
ἀρνέομαι, ἀρνήσομαι, ἡρνησάμην, _____, ἤρνημαι, _____,
    I deny

154

ἄρτι,
    adv., now
ἄρτος, ὁ,
    bread
ἀρχή, ἡ,
    beginning
ἀρχιερεύς, -έως, ὁ,
    chief-priest
ἄρχω, ἄρξω, ἦρξα, ——, ——, ——,
    I rule (*middle voice*, I begin)
ἄρχων, ἄρχοντος, ὁ,
    ruler
αὐτός, ή, ό,
    he, she, it
ἀφίημι, ἀφήσω, ἀφῆκα, ἀφεῖκα, ἀφεῖμαι, ἀφείθην,
    I forgive
ἄχρι,
    prep. with gen., until

βάθος, βάθους, τό,
    depth
βαίνω, βήσομαι, ἔβην, βέβηκα, ——, ἐβήθην (deponent),
    I go
βάλλω, βαλῶ, ἔβαλον, βέβληκα, βέβλημαι, ἐβλήθην,
    I throw, cast
βαπτίζω, βαπτίσω, ἐβάπτισα, ——, βεβάπτισμαι, ἐβαπτίσθην,
    I baptize
βασιλεία, ἡ,
    kingdom
βασιλεύς, -έως, ὁ,
    king
βασιλικός, ή, όν,
    royal, kingly
βιβλίον, τό,
    book
βίος, ὁ,
    life
βλέπω, βλέψω, ἔβλεψα, ——, ——, ——,
    I see

γάμος ὁ,
    marriage, marriage feast

γάρ,
    conj., for
γεννάω, γεννήσω, ἐγέννησα, γεγέννηκα, γεγέννημαι, ἐγεννήθην
    I beget
γένος, γένους, τό,
    race
γίνομαι, γενήσομαι, ἐγενόμην, γέγονα, γεγένημαι, ἐγενήθην,
    I become
γινώσκω, γνώσομαι, ἔγνων, ἔγνωκα, ἔγνωσμαι, ἐγνώσθην,
    I know
γλῶσσα, ἡ,
    tongue, language
γνῶσις, γνώσεως, ἡ,
    knowledge
γραμματεύς, -έως, ὁ,
    scribe
γραφή, ἡ,
    writing, Scripture
γράφω, γράψω, ἔγραψα, γέγραφα, γέγραμμαι, ἐγράφην,
    I write

δαιμόνιον, τό,
    demon
δέ,
    conj., but, moreover, and
δέχομαι, δέξομαι, ἐδεξάμην, _____, δέδεγμαι, ἐδέχθην,
    I receive
δηλόω, δηλώσω, ἐδήλωσα, _____, _____, ἐδηλώθην,
    I show, make manifest
διά,
    prep.; with gen., through; with abl., by, through; with acc., because
    of, on account of
διδάσκαλος, ὁ,
    teacher
διδάσκω, διδάξω, ἐδίδαξα, _____, _____, ἐδιδάχθην,
    I teach
διδαχή, ἡ,
    teaching
δίδωμι, δώσω, ἔδωκα, δέδωκα, δέδομαι, ἐδόθην,
    I give
δικαιοσύνη, ἡ,
    righteousness

διώκω, διώξω, ἐδίωξα, _____, δεδίωγμαι, ἐδιώχθην,
    I persecute
δόξα, ἡ,
    praise
δοξάζω, δοξάσω, ἐδόξασα, _____, δεδόξασμαι, ἐδοξάσθην,
    I glorify
δοῦλος, ὁ,
    slave, servant
δύναμις, δυνάμεως, ἡ,
    power
δῶρον, τό,
    gift

ἐάν,
    cond. particle with subjunctive, if
ἐαυτοῦ, ἧς, οὖ,
    of himself, of herself, of itself
ἐγγίζω, ἐγγίσω, ἤγγισα, ἤγγικα, _____, _____,
    I come near, draw near
ἐγείρω, ἐγερῶ, ἤγειρα, _____, ἐγήγερμαι, ἠγέρθην,
    I raise up
ἐγώ,
    I
ἔθνος, ἔθνους, τό,
    nation (plural, gentiles)
ἔθος, ἔθους, τό,
    custom
εἰ,
    cond. particle with indicative, if, since
εἶδον, 2nd aorist of ὁράω,
    I saw
εἰμί, ἔσομαι,
    I am
εἶπον, 2nd aorist of λέγω or φημί,
    I said
εἰρήνη, ἡ,
    peace
εἰς
    prep. with acc., into, unto, because of
ἐκ, (ἐξ before a vowel),
    prep. with abl., out of, from
ἐκεῖνος, η, ο,
    that

157

ἐκκλησία, ἡ,
  church
ἔλεος, ἐλέους, το,
  mercy
ἐλπίς, ἐλπίδος, ἡ,
  hope
ἐμαυτοῦ, ῆς, οῦ,
  of myself
ἐμός, ἐμή, ἐμόν,
  my
ἐν,
  prep. with loc., in, on; with inst., by
ἐντολή, ἡ,
  commandment
ἐπαγγέλλομαι, _____, ἐπηγγειλάμην, _____, ἐπήγγελμαι, _____,
  I announce
ἐπαγγελία, ἡ,
  promise
ἐπί,
  with gen., upon, on, at, by (*emphasizing contact*)
  with loc., upon, on, at, over (*emphasizing position*)
  with acc., upon, on, to, up to (*emphasizing direction or motion*)
ἐπιθυμία, ἡ,
  lust, desire
ἔργον, τό,
  work
ἔρημος, ἡ,
  desert
ἔρχομαι, ἐλεύσομαι, ἦλθον, ἐλήλυθα, _____, _____,
  I come, go
  ἀπέρχομαι,
    I go away
  διέρχομαι,
    I go through
  εἰσέρχομαι,
    I go into, enter
  ἐξέρχομαι,
    I go out
  κατέρχομαι,
    I go down
  συνέρχομαι,
    I come together

ἐσθίω, φάγομαι, ἔφαγον, _____, _____, _____,
  I eat

ἔσχατος, η, ον
   last
ἕτερος, α, ον,
   other (*usually another of a different kind*)
ἔτι,
   still, yet
ἑτοιμάζω, ἑτοιμάσω, ἡτοίμασα, ἡτοίμακα, ἡτοίμασμαι, ἡτοιμάσθην,
   I prepare
εὐαγγελίζομαι, ⸺, εὐηγγέλισα, ⸺, εὐηγγέλισμαι, εὐηγγελίσθην,
   I preach the gospel
εὐαγγέλιον, τό,
   gospel
εὐλογέω, εὐλογήσω, εὐλόγησα, εὐλόγηκα, εὐλόγημαι, εὐλογήθην,
   I bless
εὐχαριστέω, εὐχαριστήσω, εὐχαρίστησα, ⸺, ⸺, εὐχαριστήθην,
   I give thanks
ἔχω, ἕξω, ἔσχον, ἔσχηκα, ⸺, ⸺, (*imperfect* εἶχον),
   I have
ἕως,
   adv., until

ζητέω, ζητήσω, ἐζήτησα, ⸺, ⸺, ⸺,
   I seek
ζωή, ἡ,
   life

ἤδη
   already
ἡμέρα, ἡ,
   day
ἡμέτερος, α, ον,
   our

θάλασσα, ἡ,
   sea
θάνατος, ὁ,
   death
θαυμάζω, θαυμάσομαι, ἐθαύμασα, ⸺, ⸺, ἐθαυμάσθην,
   I wonder
θέλημα, θελήματος, τό,
   will
θέλω, θελήσω, ἠθέλησα, ⸺, ⸺, ⸺, (*imp.,* ἤθελον),
   I wish

159

θεός, ὁ,
  god, God
θεραπεύω, θεραπεύσω, ἐθεράπευσα, _____, τεθεράπευμαι, ἐθεραπεύθην,
  I heal
θεωρέω, θεωρήσω, ἐθεώρησα, _____, _____, _____,
  I behold
θυγάτηρ, θυγατρός, ἡ,
  daughter

ἴδιος, α, ον,
  his own, her own, its own
ἱερεύς, ἱερέως, ὁ,
  priest
ἱερόν, τό,
  temple
Ἰησοῦς, ὁ,
  Jesus
ἱλασμός, ὁ,
  propitiation
ἵνα,
  conj., usually with subjunctive, in order that, that
ἵστημι, στήσω, ἔστησα, (or ἔστην), ἕστηκα _____, ἐστάθην,
  I cause to stand, I stand
ἰσχυρός, ά, όν,
  strong, sufficient
ἰχθύς, ἰχθύος, ὁ,
  fish

καθαρίζω, καθαριῶ, ἐκαθάρισα, _____, _____, ἐκαθαρίσθην,
  I cleanse, I purify
καθώς,
  comparative particle, just as, even as
καί,
  conj., and, also, even (καί . . . καί, both . . . and)
καινός, ή, όν,
  new
κακός, ή, όν,
  bad
καλέω, καλέσω, ἐκάλησα, κέκληκα, κέκλημαι, ἐκλήθην,
  I call
καλός, ή, όν,
  good
καρδία, ἡ,
  heart

καρπός, ὁ,
    fruit
κατά,
    prep.; with abl., down from; *with gen.,* down upon; *with acc.,*
    according to, along
καταβαίνω,
    I go down
κηρύσσω, κηρύξω, ἐκήρυξα, _____, _____, ἐκηρύχθην,
    I preach, proclaim
κοινωνία, ἡ,
    fellowship
κόσμος, ὁ,
    world
κρίμα, κρίματος, τό
    judgment
κρίνω, κρινῶ, ἔκρινα, κέκρικα, κέκριμαι, ἐκρίθην,
    I judge
κρίσις, κρίσεως, ἡ,
    judgment
κύριος, ὁ,
    lord, Lord

λαλέω, λαλήσω, ἐλάλησα, λελάληκα, λελάλημαι, ἐλαλήθην,
    I speak
λαμβάνω, λήμψομαι, ἔλαβον, εἴληφα, εἴλημμαι, ἐλήμφθην,
    I take, I receive
λαός, ὁ,
    people
λέγω, ἐρῶ, εἶπον, εἴρηκα, εἴρημαι, ἐρρέθην (or ἐρρήθην),
    I say
λείπω, λείψω, ἔλιπον, _____, λέλειμμαι, ἐλείφθην,
    I leave
λίθος, ὁ,
    stone
λόγος, ὁ,
    word, discourse
λοιπός, ή, όν,
    remaining (οἱ λοιποί, the rest)
λύω, λύσω, ἔλυσα, λέλυκα, λέλυμαι, ἐλύθην,
    I loose, destroy

μαθητής, ὁ,
    disciple

μακάριος, α, ον,
    blessed
μαρτυρία, ἡ,
    witness, testimony
μέγας, μεγάλη, μέγα,
    great
μέν,
    exclamatory particle, indeed (μέν . . . δέ, strong adversative, on the
    one hand . . . on the other hand)
μένω, μενῶ, ἔμεινα, μεμένηκα, ———, ———,
    I remain, abide
Μεσσίας, ὁ,
    Messiah
μετά,
    prep. with gen., with; with acc., after
μή,
    usual negative with moods other than the indicative, not
μηδέ,
    negative conjunction, but not, nor (μηδέ . . . μηδέ, neither . . . nor)
μηδείς, μηδεμία, μηδέν,
    no one
μηκέτι,
    negative adverb, not yet, no longer
μήτηρ, μητρός, ἡ,
    mother
μικρός, ά, όν,
    little, small
μισέω, μισήσω, ἐμίσησα, μεμίσηκα, ———, ———,
    I hate, detest
μόνος, η, ον,
    only, alone

νεανίσκος, ὁ,
    young man
νεκρός, ά, όν,
    dead
νικάω, νικήσω, ἐνίκησα, νενίκηκα, ———, ———,
    I overcome, conquer
νόμος, ὁ,
    law
νύξ, νυκτός, ἡ,
    night
νῦν,
    adv., now

162

ὁ, ἡ, τό,
the
ὁδός, ἡ,
way, road
ὅθεν,
adv., whence
οἶδα,
(*perf. form of obsolete* εἴδω, used as present), I know
οἰκία, ἡ,
house
οἶκος, ὁ,
house
ὅλος, η, ον,
whole
ὁμολογέω, ὁμολογήσω, ὡμολόγησα, ____, ____, ____,
I profess, confess
ὄνομα, ὀνόματος, τό,
name
ὁράω, ὄψομαι, εἶδον ἑώρακα (*or* ἑόρακα), ____, ὤφθην,
I see
ὄρος, ὄρους, τό,
mountain
ὅς, ἥ, ὅ,
who, which
ὅστις, ἥτις ὅτι,
who, which (*qualitative in force*)
ὅτι,
conj., because, that
οὐ
(οὐκ *before vowel;* οὐχ *before vowel with rough breathing*), *usual negative with indicative mood,* not
οὐδέ,
negative conjunction, and not, nor (οὐδέ . . . οὐδέ, neither . . . nor
οὐδείς, οὐδεμία, οὐδέν,
no one
οὐκέτι,
negative adverb, no longer
οὔπω,
negative adverb, not yet
οὐρανός, ὁ,
heaven
οὖς, ὠτός, τό,
ear

163

οὗτος, αὕτη, τοῦτο,
  this
οὕτως,
  adv., thus, so, in this manner
ὀφείλω,
  I owe, ought
ὀφθαλμός, ὁ,
  eye
ὄχλος, ὁ,
  multitude

παλαιός, ά, όν,
  old
παρά
  prep.; with abl., from; *with loc.*, before, beside; *with acc.*, beside,
  beyond, along
παραβολή, ἡ,
  parable
παρακαλέω,
  I exhort, beseech, comfort
παράκλητος, ὁ,
  comforter
παρρησία, ἡ,
  boldness
παρουσία, ἡ,
  presence, coming
πᾶς, πᾶσα, πᾶν,
  all, every, the whole
πάσχω, ——, ἔπαθον, πέπονθα, ——, ——,
  I suffer
πατήρ, πατρός, ὁ,
  father
πέμπω, πέμψω, ἔπεμψα, ——, ——, ἐπέμφθην,
  I send
περί,
  prep; with gen., about, concerning; *with acc.*, about, around
περιπατέω, περιπατήσω, περιεπάτησα, περιπεπάτηκα, ——, ——,
  I walk
πίνω, πίομαι, ἔπιον, πέπωκα, ——, ἐπόθην,
  I drink
πίπτω, πεσοῦμαι, ἔπεσον, πέπτωκα, ——, ——,
  I fall
πιστεύω, πιστεύσω, ἐπίστευσα, πεπίστευκα, πεπίστευμαι, ἐπιστεύθην,
  I believe

πίστις, πίστεως, ἡ,
    faith
πιστός, ἡ, όν,
    faithful
πλανάω, πλανήσω, ἐπλάνησα, _____, πεπλάνημαι, ἐπλανήθην,
    I lead astray, deceive
πλοῖον, τό,
    boat
πνεῦμα, πνεύματος, τό,
    spirit
ποιέω, ποιήσω, ἐποίησα, πεποίηκα, πεποίημαι,
    I do, make
πόλις, πόλεως ἡ,
    city
πολύς, πολλή, πολύ,
    much
πονηρός, ά, όν,
    evil
πορεύομαι, πορεύσομαι, ἐπορευσάμην, _____, πεπόρευμαι, ἐπορεύθην,
    I go
πρίν,
    adv., before
πρό,
    prep. with abl., before
πρός,
    prep.; with loc., at; *with acc.*, to, toward, with, at
προσεύχομαι, προσεύξομαι, προσηυξάμην, _____, _____, _____,
    I pray
προφήτης, ὁ,
    prophet
πρῶτος, η, ον,
    first

ῥῆμα, ῥήματος, τό,
    word, saying

σάρξ, σαρκός, ἡ,
    flesh
σεαυτοῦ, σεαυτῆς,
    of yourself
σκάνδαλον, τό,
    offense, stumbling-block
σκοτία, ἡ,
    darkness

σκότος, σκότους, τό,
  darkness
σός, σή, σόν,
  your own (*sec., per., sing.*)
σπείρω, ———, ἔσπειρα ———, ———, ———,
  I sow
στάσις, στάσεως, ἡ,
  strife, dissension
σταυρόω, σταυρώσω, ἐσταύρωσα, ———, ἐσταύρωμαι, ἐσταυρώθην,
  I crucify
στάχυς, στάχυος, τό,
  corn, ear of corn
στόμα, στόματος, τό,
  mouth
στρατιώτης, ὁ,
  soldier
σύ,
  you
σύν,
  prep., with ins. with, together with
συνάγω,
  I gather together
συναγωγή, ἡ,
  synagogue
σώζω, σώσω, ἔσωσα, σέσωκα, σέσωσμαι, ἐσώθην,
  I save
σῶμα, σώματος, τό,
  body
σωτηρία, ἡ,
  salvation

τέκνον, τό,
  child
τελειόω, ———, ἐτελείωσα, τετελείωκα, τετελείωμαι, ἐτελειώθην,
  I perfect, I carry out to an end
τέλος, τέλους, τό,
  end
τηρέω, τηρήσω, ἐτήρησα, τετήρηκα, τετήρημαι, ἐτηρήθην,
  I keep
τίθημι, θήσω, ἔθηκα, τέθεικα, τέθειμαι, ἐτέθην,
  I place, put
τιμάω, τιμήσω, ἐτίμησα, ———, τετίμημαι, ———,
  I honor

166

τίς, τί,
   who?, what?
τις, τι,
   someone, something, a certain one
τόπος, ὁ,
   place
τότε,
   adv., then
τυφλός, ὁ,
   blind man
τυφλόω, ———, ἐτύφλωσα, τετύφλωκα, ———, ———,
   I blind, make blind

ὕδωρ, ὕδατος, τό,
   water
υἱός, ὁ,
   son
ὑμέτερος, α, ον,
   your (*sec. per., pl.*)
ὑπάγω,
   I go away
ὑπέρ,
   prep.; with abl., in behalf of, instead of; *with acc.*, over, above,
   beyond
ὑπό,
   prep.; with abl., by (*agency*); *with acc.*, under

φαίνω, φανοῦμαι, ———, ———, ———, ἐφάνην,
   I shine
φανερόω, φανερώσω, ἐφανέρωσα, ———, πεφανέρωμαι, ἐφανερώθην,
   I make manifest
φέρω, οἴσω, ἤνεγκα (*or* ἤνεγκον), ἐνήνοχα, ———, ἠνέχθην,
   I bring, bear
φιλέω, ———, ἐφίλησα, πεφίληκα, ———, ———, ———,
   I love
φωνή, ἡ,
   voice
φῶς, φωτός, τό,
   light

χαρά, ἡ,
   joy

χάρις, χάριτος, ἡ,
    grace, thanks
χείρ, χειρός, ἡ,
    hand
χρεία, ἡ,
    need
χρίσμα, χρίσματος, τό,
    anointing
Χριστός, ὁ,
    Christ

ψεύδομαι, ——, ἐψευσάμην, ——, ——, ——,
    I lie, deceive
ψεῦδος, ψεύδους, τό,
    lie
ψεύστης, ὁ,
    liar

ὥρα, ἡ,
    hour
ὡς,
    comparative particle, as, like

INDEX

(Numbers refer to paragraphs and their subdivisions.)

169

	DATE DUE		